Nascent Entrepreneurship: Empirical Studies and Developments

Nascent Entrepreneurship: Empirical Studies and Developments

Empirical Studies and Developments

Developments

Per Davidsson

Brisbane Graduate School of Business,
QUT, Australia
and
Jönköping International Business School, Sweden
per.davidsson@qut.edu.au

the essence of knowledge
Boston – Delft

Foundations and Trends® in Entrepreneurship

Published, sold and distributed by:
now Publishers Inc.
PO Box 1024
Hanover, MA 02339
USA
Tel. +1 (781) 871 0245
www.nowpublishers.com
sales@nowpublishers.com

Outside North America:
now Publishers Inc.
PO Box 179
2600 AD Delft
The Netherlands
Tel. +31-6-51115274

A Cataloging-in-Publication record is available from the Library of Congress.

Printed on acid-free paper

ISBN: 1-933019-20-4; ISSNs: Paper version 1551-3114; Electronic version 1551-3122
© 2006 P. Davidsson

Contents

Section 1   Introduction   **1**

Section 2   Person Factors Leading to Nascent
                Entrepreneur Status   **5**

2.1   Resources in terms of human, social and
      financial capital   6
2.2   Motivations and perceptions   8
2.3   Other person factors   9
2.4   Conclusion   10

Section 3   The Discovery Process   **13**

3.1   Characteristics of the discovery process   13
3.2   Process characteristics and outcomes   15
3.3   Conclusion   16

Section 4   The Exploitation Process   **19**

4.1   Factors leading to successful exploitation   20

4.2   Process characteristics   22
4.3   Process characteristics and outcomes   23
4.4   Process characteristics and outcomes for various subgroups of
       NEs   28
4.5   Conclusion   30

Section 5   Some Particular Themes   **33**

5.1   Characteristics and dynamics of new venture teams   33
5.2   Gender   36
5.3   Ethnicity   38
5.4   Growth aspirations   39

Section 6   The Bigger Picture   **43**

Section 7   Developments So Far   **47**

7.1   An atheoretical research endeavor?   47
7.2   Increased theoretical sophistication   48
7.3   Increased methodological sophistication   50

Section 8   Further Development Needs   **55**

Section 9   Conclusion   **67**

References   **69**

1

Introduction

This article reviews the extant empirical literature on 'nascent entrepreneurship', takes stock of its findings as well as theoretical and methodological developments, and concludes by developing suggestions for future research in this area. This is in the hope that such a review and stock-taking will assist researchers in making the best use of extant data sets on 'nascent entrepreneurship' and in designing future studies on this topic.

As far as this author has been able to determine, the term 'nascent entrepreneur' first appeared in the research literature in a method orientated conference paper in 1992 [114]. The closely related concept 'nascent venture' first appeared in a journal article published the same year [112]. It is, of course, no happenstance that both works are lead authored by Paul Reynolds, who undoubtedly has been the main driving force behind the major, empirical research programs in this area. (cf. [43]). Another important influence that has brought the idea of studying on-going start-ups to empirical realization is Gartner's (and collaborators') calls for a re-orientation of entrepreneurship research from characteristics of individuals to *behaviors* in the *process of emergence* ([59], [60]; [61]; [83]). Other influential scholars' early emphasis on the *process* nature of new venture creation are additional but more indirect sources of inspiration that have helped giving shape to this branch of research ([15]; [31]; [138]; [141]).

The key ideas behind the empirical study of 'nascent entrepreneurs' – or 'firms in gestation' – are the following: First, the research aims to identify a statistically representative sample of on-going venture start-up efforts. Second, in some projects, these start-up efforts are subsequently followed over time through repeated waves of data collection so that insights can be gained also into process issues and determinants of outcomes. This research approach is a central development in entrepreneurship research, and, arguably, one of the greatest contributions this line of research can make to social science in general. This is so for the following reasons:

(1) The approach aims to overcome the *under-coverage of the smallest and youngest entities* and the *non-comparability* across countries that typically signify available business data bases from statistical organizations. Overcoming under coverage and non-comparability allows describing and comparing the prevalence of entrepreneurial activity in different economies. The more comprehensive studies of nascent entrepreneurs also aim to overcome the *lack of data* on many interesting variables that also restrict the usefulness of 'secondary' data sets.

(2) The approach also aims to overcome the *selection bias* resulting from including only start-up efforts that actually resulted in up-and-running businesses. This is achieved by screening a very large, probabilistic sample of households or individuals in order to identify those who are currently involved in an on-going start-up effort. The potential criticality of this is demonstrated by the fact that studying only those processes that result in successfully established firms is equivalent to studying gambling by exclusively investigating winners.[1]

---

[1] From such a study one would, among other things, conclude that (a) gambling is profitable (for the gamblers); (b) the more you bet, the more you win; and (c) the higher risks you take (i.e., the more unlikely winners you pick), the more you win. While true for winners these conclusions are, of course, blatantly false for the population of gamblers (cf. the population of start-up attempts) ([38], [42]).

(3) The approach further aims to overcome *hindsight bias* and *memory decay* resulting from asking survey questions about the start-up process retrospectively, and to get the *temporal order of measurement* right for causal analysis.

The first of these points is a main rationale for the repeated cross-sectional surveys in the *Global Entrepreneurship Monitor* studies (GEM) (e.g., [106]; [107]; [108]; [109]; [110]; [111]) while the third point is a key reason for carrying out the US-based *Panel Study of Entrepreneurial Dynamics* (PSED) ([64]; [105]) and its likewise longitudinal counterpart studies in various other countries, each of which has followed several hundred start-up efforts over 12 to 72 months. The second point above is, arguably, of central interest for both types of effort.

The purpose of this paper is to take stock of the developments of 'nascent entrepreneur' – or 'firm gestation' – research so far, and to suggest directions for future research efforts along those lines. For this purpose, over 75 journal articles, book chapters, conference papers and research reports from the PSED; its international counterpart studies; scholarly articles based on the GEM data, and a number of reports from the Danish and German extensions of the GEM were reviewed by the author. With regards to scholarly work based on these data sets the intention has been to be as complete as possible[2]. To a lesser extent reference will be made to policy reports and to other empirical work on organizational emergence, which has been conducted outside of these major research programs. The review generated 135 citations-supported claims concerning NE research results to date in the first draft of this paper. The accuracy of these claims was subsequently cross-checked by a research-trained assistant and instances of possible misrepresentation of the original works were carefully noted. This led the author to revise the original claims in a handful of instances, whereas in a few

---

[2] The form of publication has not been heavily weighted in this review. This is because (a) much of this research is still on-going and many manuscripts have as yet not reached their 'final destination', and (b) the pressure and/or inclination to take one's findings to (prestigious) journal outlets is much lesser in many countries outside the US, so it is a false inference to assume that all high quality work will appear in (prestigious) journals and that all work that does not is of questionable quality. As regards doctoral dissertations these are considered published and finalised works (with ISBN etc.) in Sweden and several other countries.

additional cases the original claims were retained after the author re-checked their accordance with the sources.

To a certain extent the author's assessment of this field of research builds also on his direct involvement as member of the Executive Committee of the *Entrepreneurship Research Consortium* (ERC) – the body that designed and initially funded PSED in the US – and as one of the principal designers and investigators of the Swedish counterpart study. While both PSED and GEM have collected data also on *nascent intrapreneurs* – those currently involved in venture start-up activities as a job assignment for an employer – the review will focus exclusively on nascent entrepreneurs, unless the research concerns comparison of the two groups or lumps them together as one category.

The review will proceed as follows. First, the thrust of the findings will be reported for the following broad areas of research topics: *Person factors leading to nascent entrepreneur status; The discovery process; The exploitation process; Some particular themes (Teams; Gender; Ethnicity, and Growth aspirations)*, and *The bigger picture* (i.e., aggregate level antecedents and effects of nascent entrepreneurship). The review will then turn to the issue of *Developments so far* – mostly in terms of increasing theoretical and methodological sophistication. Finally, *Further development needs* will be thoroughly discussed, and a considerable set of specific propositions will be made regarding improvements that can be made in future research efforts within this general research approach. Although the research potential of the current PSED and GEM data sets has been far from exhausted at this point, and while some recommendations can be fruitfully applied to analysis of extant data, they are largely written with entirely new empirical projects in mind.[3]

---

[3] For example, at the time of this writing a US-based 'PSED II' is under development and in Australia an application for a comprehensive, PSED-like research program has just been approved.

2

Person Factors Leading to Nascent Entrepreneur Status

A common approach in early entrepreneurship research was to compare 'entrepreneurs' – understood as business founders or small business owner-managers – with a comparison group of employed managers or the general population (e.g., [19]; [134]). One of the problems with this approach is that if a difference is found it is not clear how it should be interpreted, because several possibilities are confounded by design (cf. [40], p. 70):

- The propensity to *engage* in entrepreneurial behavior. Those with higher propensity should, *ceteris paribus*, have a higher likelihood of ending up in the 'entrepreneur' sample.

- The ability to *succeed* in such behavior. Those who are successful in entrepreneurial endeavors should, *ceteris paribus*, have a higher likelihood of still being members of the group sampled as 'entrepreneurs' and therefore end up in that sample.

- The propensity to *persist* in the face of failure. Those who try again, or stay in business despite sub-standard performance (cf. [66]) should, *ceteris paribus*, have a higher likelihood of ending up in the 'entrepreneur' sample.

- A range of *situational factors* (i.e., not fundamentally person-based) that contribute to engaging, succeeding or persisting in entrepreneurship.

The comprehensive, 'early catch', longitudinal PSED design presents an excellent opportunity to disentangle some of these issues. For example, as will be demonstrated further below, entry versus process differences by gender and ethnicity have interesting implications. As will also be discussed below, however, the 'failure' issue is not as straightforward as it might first seem, which is something the PSED research has helped revealing. In this section the focus will be limited to characteristics of those who enter into a start-up process. Compared with earlier research this avoids confounding of the first two points above and to some extent also the fourth one. Subsequent sections concerning process issues address also the third point.

2.1. Resources in terms of human, social and financial capital

As regards Human Capital (HC), the PSED and GEM type studies consistently find a positive effect of *level of education* on the probability to become a nascent entrepreneur (NE). The shape of the relationship differs somewhat between analyses. Swedish results ([45]; [50]) indicate positive effects along the whole spectrum or towards the high end of education, whereas US and international-comparative analyses more emphasize under representation of those with low education, with no further increase in the propensity to become NE above medium levels of education ([84]; [104]; [109]). Based on German REM data, Wagner [145] even reports lower NE prevalence for the highest education groups compared to medium levels. On the other hand, Arenius and De Clerk [9], who use GEM data from Belgium and Finland, find that those with post-secondary education are significantly more likely than those with lower education to agree that 'in the next six months there would be good opportunities for starting a business in the area where I live' (i.e., a different dependent variable than NE status). The resolution of this apparent contradiction may be that those with higher education also have better non-entrepreneurial opportunities and therefore are less likely to act upon the entrepreneurial opportunities they perceive.

Where included, previous self-employment or *experience of starting one's own firm* typically come out with positive effects ([34]; [45]; [50]; [84]). *Industry experience* has not been studied much (possibly because of difficulties attributing the nascent ventures to industries at early stages), while previous *management experience* as well as *years of work experience* seem to have weak or uncertain influence on the propensity to become NE ([6]; [34]; [45]; [50]; [84]). Wagner [143] reports that *breadth* of education and experience both are of importance, echoing a finding that was highlighted in one of the early classics in entrepreneurship research [133]. In another work, Wagner [144] reports that *work experience in young and small firms* has a positive effect on NE status. This effect is also apparent in early works (e.g., [134]) but Wagner's ascribing it to the combination of smallness and newness rather than to either dimension separately is a new addition. Finally, analyses of GEM data have suggested very strong effects of self-reported *confidence in having the relevant skills* for running one's own business ([10]; [109]; [145]); cf. the theoretical concept of *self-efficacy* ([13]; [29]). All in all there is considerable evidence that higher levels of relevant human capital, as indicated by education, experience, and self-reported skill increases individuals' propensity to engage in venture start-up processes.

There is also evidence that Social Capital (SC) is important for this decision. Swedish results indicate separate positive effects for having parents or friends and relatives, respectively, who are self-employed; direct encouragement from such role models; having worked in parents' firms; and the number of firms parents have run ([45]; [50]; [51]; cf. [37]). Cross-national analyses of GEM data suggest that those who know others who are self-employed are more than twice as likely to become NEs themselves ([10]; [109]; [145]). The importance of such factors appear much weaker or non-existent in present-day US ([6]; [39]), although Kim *et al.* [84] found a positive effect of the percentage of relatives who were self-employed.

It is somewhat debatable whether the effects of the above-mentioned indicators reflect social or human capital effects. For example, Kim *et al.* [84] attribute the effect to the HC category. It is also possible that working in parents' firms [51] contributes more to human than to social capital. Another Swedish result that questions the social capital hypothesis is the finding that those who have lived for a shorter time in their current county are over represented among NEs [50]. Presumably, those who have lived longer in the same place should have more social capital to draw upon, at least in the local environment.

As regards Financial Capital the main finding to date is that indicators of income and household net worth are not or only weakly related to the propensity to become NE. In three closely related papers based on US PSED data, Aldrich and Kim [6], Crosa *et al.* [34] and Kim *et al.* [84], respectively, found no significant effects of such variables. Reynolds [104] found the same in a US forerunner to the PSED. Across GEM countries a modest over representation has been reported for the highest third on household income ([109]; [145]), which is also what Delmar and Davidsson [50] report for Sweden. Arenius and Minniti [10], on the other hand, found some evidence for a U-shaped relationship across countries, but this effect disappeared in the presence of other variables. In a similar vein, Grilo and Thurik [69] point out the lack of any discriminative effect of perceived lack of financial support as the most striking result of their analysis of multi-country data from the *Entrepreneurship Flash Eurobarometer.*

All in all, the relationship between financial capital and propensity to become NE is likely to be far more complex than a simple, linear, positive effect. This is probably partly due to the simultaneous existence of *opportunity-based* and *necessity-based* entrepreneurship [107], which also leads to unemployment sometimes being positively related to NE status [104] although the unemployed hardly have the best financial capital situation for successfully starting a new venture.

2.2. Motivations and perceptions

It has already been noted above that those who have more confidence in their start-up related skills are much more likely to become nascent entrepreneurs. Other perceptual variables from the GEM studies have also shown considerable differences between NEs and a comparison group. This goes for, e.g., *fear of failure* (lower among NEs), *economic outlook* for family and country (more positive among NEs), and (somewhat circular, perhaps) *perception of opportunity* ([10]; [109]; [145]).

Carter, Gartner, Shaver, and Gatewood [24] took a deeper look into the stated *career reasons* of NEs and non-NEs in the US PSED. More specifically, their analysis concerns the importance of (1) self-realization, (2) financial success, (3) assuming roles, (4) innovation, (5) recognition, and (6) independence. The results are interesting and highlight the importance – for getting a realistic view of the phenomenon of business creation as a whole – of (a) looking at the entire population rather than only at the 'high end' of it, and (b) comparing with other careers. First, although there are widespread beliefs that business founders are innovative and financially motivated, there are no group differences on these dimensions. Neither are there any differences for self-realization or independence; dimensions that frequently seem to signify business founders in studies lacking a comparison group ([17]; [125]). Further, despite repeated results (cf. above) on the importance of role models for going into self-employment it is actually less the case for NEs than for the comparison group that they follow role expectations. The NEs also score lower on (need for external) recognition. To some extent these two results support a 'rebel' theory of entrepreneurship: there is some tendency for NEs – relative to others – to break away from well-trodden paths, and to care less about what others think about that. In all, Carter *et al.*'s [24] results are interesting. To the best of this author's knowledge these issues have not yet been analyzed in PSED's international counterpart studies.

2.3. Other person factors

One of the clearest results across countries is the under representation of women among NEs (e.g., [10]; [45]; [50]; [104]; [109]; [145]). The gender issue will be further discussed in a separate section further below, as will ethnicity. Other recurring results are a negative or curvilinear effect of *age*, often with a peak in the 25–34 age bracket ([50]; [104]). Other variables such as household size; marital status, family size, et cetera, have not yielded consistent results across countries.

2.4. Conclusion

Somewhat pessimistically, Wagner ([145], p. 14) asks 'What do we learn from these studies that attempt to identify factors that are important for becoming a nascent entrepreneur?' and goes on to answer 'In my view, not too much.' Pointing at the regional level research reported by Reynolds, Storey, and Westhead [113] as a positive example, the most important reason for his pessimism is that lack of harmonization of analyses and theoretical interpretation, which gives a patchy and confusing view of the relationships. To a certain extent the present author shares Wagner's limited enthusiasm for the person-factor research reported above, but mainly for different reasons. First, it was already (believed to be) known from extensive, previous research on established business founders that no person factors are very strong determinants of getting into an entrepreneurial career, and that the factors discussed above were at least of some importance. Second, the PSED design is not necessarily ideal for comparing 'entrepreneurs' – as a group of individuals who are assumed to have some differential innate characteristics – to other groups. Nascent entrepreneurs are not novice entrepreneurs; many of them do it for the second, third or nth time. It is really the venture that is 'nascent', not the person. Moreover, research suggests that roughly one third of the human population in Western countries is at some stage of their life directly involved in an independent business venture [50]. 'Nascent entrepreneur' is a temporary state. What all this means is that comparing NEs to others is somewhat akin to comparing 'holiday makers' to other people – some of whom will obviously be on holiday in the next time period. Thus, in terms of comparison of groups it may be argued that the basic logic of the design is better suited for studying 'How does being involved in a start-up process affect the person?' rather than for 'What attributes of persons make them enter a start-up process?'

However, as explained in the introduction to this section on person factors the design used in previous studies potentially confounds several different types of effects. So if the PSED/GEM type research has not revealed many new 'truths' but mostly confirms what has been reported in earlier studies about person factors increasing the probability of starting one's own firm, this was confirmation that was needed. Without it the debate could go on forever as to whether group differences represented differences concerning the propensity to *engage, succeed,* or *persist* in entrepreneurial endeavors – or method artifacts resulting from hindsight bias or memory decay. The results so far indicate that interpreting results from previous research as reflecting the 'engage' dimensions has not been entirely wrong, saving the entrepreneurship research community from a need for major re-interpretation of what it thought was known.

In addition, the results reported so far do not completely lack novelty. For example, Carter *et al.*'s [24] comparative results on motivation for becoming NE definitely seem to deviate from what was previously thought to be known, making the motivations of business founders seem much less unique to that career choice. If confirmed in future analyses comparing NEs with those pursuing other careers this will be an area where research on nascent entrepreneurs changed the received view of what leads to business creation.

3

The Discovery Process

PSED data from the US and Scandinavia have been used for analyses of the discovery process, i.e., the origins of the business idea and how different ways of finding and developing business ideas shape the fate of the venture. As longitudinal, representative sample data have not been available before it is natural that much of what has been presented to date concerning the process is descriptive in nature. However, there are also examples of theory testing and of efforts to relate characteristics of the discovery process to subsequent outcomes.

3.1. Characteristics of the discovery process

A good empirical starting point for this section is Hills and Singh's [72] basic 'fact finding' about the discovery process. They note that about 1/3 of the NEs in the US PSED say they engaged in 'deliberate search' for a business opportunity. The share who agrees that 'the best ideas just come' is also about 1/3, whereas more than 2/3 agree that finding a business opportunity 'has involved several learning steps over time, rather than a one time event'. That is, a majority sees opportunity identification as a process. This is important in relation to theorizing à la Kirzner [87], where discovery is portrayed as an instantaneous flash of insight. Based on Bhave's [15] distinction between 'internally' and 'externally' triggered opportunity identification the PSED mail questionnaire included a question concerning what came first: the wish to go into business for oneself, or the specific venture idea. In the US PSED 37% of NEs say the idea came first, while 42% say the wish to start one's own firm came first, and 21% claim these were simultaneous events [72]. This indicates a relatively high frequency of Bhave's [15] less textbook-like 'internally stimulated' process. The latter type of process often starts with individuals identifying and solving problems for themselves, only to eventually realize that others have the same problem and that their willingness to pay for having it solved presents a business opportunity for those who can solve it. Somewhat inconsistently, however, the proportion contemplating only one idea is 27.8% according to the same data set. With the high proportion of 'internally stimulated' discovery processes one would have expected this number to be even higher. Unpublished analyses of the Swedish data conducted by the author suggest an even lower occurrence, less than 20%, of processes starting with the wish to start one's own firm, and over 50% saying the idea clearly came first. In all, it is clear from these results that in a large number of cases the process never includes a step consisting of the screening and choice among a number of *different* venture ideas (or 'opportunities').

Based on PSED-inspired research on new *internal* ventures in a large cohort of young, independent firms (which was used as a screening sample for emerging internal ventures), Chandler, Dahlqvist, and Davidsson ([26], [27]) used 16 items and cluster analysis to arrive at three relatively distinct and readily interpretable types of discovery processes: *proactive search, reactive search*, and *fortuitous discovery*. In their sample the first category was the most common, having the same frequency as the other two combined. This easily leads to the speculation that search in established firms would be more systematic than in emerging firms. However, Honig [75] found no difference in the Swedish PSED between NEs and nascent *intrapreneurs* (NIs; those who are involved in a venture start-up for their employers) in the proportion having engaged in systematic search. The figure arrived at, 21%, is more than ten percentage points lower than what Hills and

Singh [72] reported for the US PSED, which is another indication of a country difference in the propensity for systematic search. Based on Norwegian data, Alsos and Kolvereid [7] compared the extent to which novice and habitual NEs carried out market research, without finding any significant difference. Neither did Alsos and Ljunggren [8] find any gender differences on the same issue.

Smith [132] derived and tested a number of specific hypotheses concerning the discovery process for codified vs. tacit venture ideas (which he operationalizes with a combination of three questions). First, he argues that codified opportunities are more frequent than tacit ones, which is confirmed. Second, he holds that people are more likely to find 'codified opportunities' through systematic search. This is also confirmed (although the testing is performed in a somewhat awkward way). Third, he holds that prior knowledge (cf. [127]) will be more likely to lead to 'tacit opportunities'. This prediction is also borne out and further supported by qualitative, case based analysis. The paper is interesting because it represents an early effort to explore and explain why and how different types of venture ideas (or 'opportunities') result from different types of discovery processes.

3.2. Process characteristics and outcomes

So far only a few papers have related discovery process characteristics to outcomes. Before reviewing this research it is useful to know what type of outcome variables have been used in this research. One type of outcome is *making (further) progress* in the start-up process. A continuous, dependent variable in this category is the *number of gestation activities* completed in subsequent periods ([45]; [119]). Another is the *self-reported status* of the venture, in terms on 'abandoned', 'dormant'; 'still trying', and 'up and running' or a collapse of these categories into a dichotomy ([22]; [53]; [57]). Another type of outcome variable is *financial performance*. Examples here include dichotomous dependent variables like achieving *first sales, positive cash flow* or *profitability* by a certain point in time ([45]; [50]; [102]) as well as continuous measures of levels of sales or profitability among those who have at all reached the market ([27]; [54]). As will be discussed later on, neither of these measures is ideal for all purposes, and several of them have severe limitations for certain types of analysis.

Hills, Lumpkin, and Baltrusaityte [71] and Baltrusaityte, Acs, and Hills [12] relate Bhave's 'internally stimulated' and 'externally stimulated' processes to various types of outcomes in terms of whether in follow-up interviews the NEs got the venture up and running; were still trying, or had abandoned it. Differences were found neither for these outcome measures nor for projected future income from the ventures. Likewise, the degree of formality of search was not related to outcomes in the US PSED data. However, those who had explored fewer ideas; had stuck to the same idea rather than changing it, and whose ideas grew out of particular industry experience, were somewhat more likely to have their firms up and running after 12 and 36 months.

Swedish PSED results relating process characteristics to making further progress in the process (measured as numbers of 'gestation activities' completed per time unit in the subsequent period) found a negative effect of systematic search, and a positive effect of incrementalism (i.e., that discovery had 'involved several learning steps over time') [76]. So far, then, the results do not speak in favor of systematic search. However, in their research on internal new ventures in young, independent firms, Chandler *et al.* [27] found that ideas identified through proactive search were implemented more rapidly than those resulting from reactive search or fortuitous discovery. After 18 months there were no significant differences in survival rates, but initiatives based on proactive search had higher sales and return on sales than the other two groups. For return on sales the effect was only marginally significant ($p < 0.10$).

3.3. Conclusion

Interesting questions regarding the discovery process have previously only been possible to address through retrospective designs with highly questionable validity, and to some extent through experimental research where the external validity can also be questioned (as can the extent to which the subjects are representative for real world entrepreneurs). As a result very little solid, empirically based knowledge exists in this

4

The Exploitation Process

While the discovery process refers to the identification and conceptual development of an idea for a venture the exploitation process refers to the tangible actions that are taken in order to realize this idea, e.g., by acquiring resources and creating demand. Before proceeding further, the reader should be reminded about the different types of outcome measures that have been used in this research: dichotomous or continuous indicators of *making (further) progress* in the start-up process, and likewise dichotomous or continuous assessment of *financial performance* among the remaining cases for which such assessment is relevant. Again, no available measure is superior for all purposes and for some there are non-negligible risks of misinterpretations. This is an issue to which there will be reason to return.

An obvious first question concerning the exploitation process is how many do at all become up and running businesses? An early indication here was the Carter *et al.* [22] forerunner to PSED, in which study 48% of the cases reported themselves as up and running businesses after 18 months. Reviewing studies employing somewhat different methodologies and period length Wagner [145] found realization rates ranging from 22 to 62%. According to his review a rather typical 12-month figure for studies employing PSED methodology seems to be around 45%. One should then note that this means within 12 months from 'first capture' into the study. One problem with the PSED design is that different ventures are caught at different stages, and some cases may have been active start-up efforts for years before being sampled, while cases that are abandoned rather quickly after initiation are, in comparison, under sampled ([38], [42]). All things considered it may still serve as a useful, rough estimate – and almost certainly subject to spatial and temporal variations – that something in the order of 33–50% of all start-up efforts result in firms that trade in the market for at least some period of time.

4.1. Factors leading to successful exploitation

Some researchers have investigated factors associated with success in the exploitation process without looking at any characteristics of the process itself. One example is Davidsson and Honig [45]. With regards to *making progress in the process* they found positive effects of indicators of *specific* rather than *general* human capital (cf. [32]; [35]). That is, business education and previous start-up experience appear helpful, while no effect was found for education level, management experience or work experience. The positive effect of previous start-up experience on outcomes has been confirmed in other analyses of Swedish, Norwegian and Dutch data ([51]; [53], [55]; [116]; [139]). Davidsson and Honig [45] also found positive effects of Social Capital indicators on making progress. However, it was in their analysis of financial outcomes that the latter type of indicators came more to the fore. In particular, linking up with a business network specifically for the purpose of furthering the start-up came out with the strongest positive effect. A suggestive general pattern in Davidsson and Honig's [45] analyses is that as the process unfolds from entry to progress and financial outcomes, the relative importance of SC to HC increases, as does the emphasis on specific (i.e., directly venturing-related) capital to general forms of capital.

Delmar and Gunnarsson [51], who also used the Swedish PSED data, found stronger support for effects of HC compared with SC. This underlines that this type of results is highly sensitive to the specific indicators used for HC and SC, as well as which specific outcome measure is used. An interesting observation based on Dutch is that the familiar positive effect of previous start-up experience is confirmed only for those who score low on other types of experience. We noted above that Wagner [143] found breadth of experience to be a predictor of NE status. More recent analyses by the same author cast doubt on this being a success factor. It may simply be a question of some people trying out many things, one of them being starting a business, without their varied experience contributing to successful outcomes [147]. On the other hand, Wagner's [147] comparison of characteristics of nascent and 'infant' entrepreneurs suggests previous *industry experience* is of considerable importance for successful completion of the process. Baltrusaityte *et al.* [12] lend some support for that notion based on US PSED data.

Analyzing Canadian PSED data, Diochon *et al.* [57] found no HC differences between NEs continuing and abandoning their projects, respectively. For SC the only significant effect concerned direct encouragement from close relatives. However, they found substantial differences for cognitive dimensions that apparently have not been analyzed in the other country studies. More specifically, those focused on 'doing things better' were more likely to continue than those focused on 'doing things differently'. Likewise, those geared towards a venture of 'manageable size' were less likely to abandon than those preferring 'to grow as large as possible'. These results indicate that those initially hoping to start innovative, high-potential ventures are more likely to give up (which is confirmed by Samuelsson [120], based on Swedish data). However, Diochon *et al.* [57] also make the important observation that most of those who abandon do so because they want to, not because they have to. This is but one aspect of the complicated nature of the dependent variable in this type of research.

We have noted above that access to financial capital had little relationship to entering into nascent entrepreneurship. The weak effect of this factor is repeated in analyses related to outcomes. Based on Canadian, Dutch and US data the conclusions have been the same ([57]; [103]; [140]). While access to financial capital may be extremely important for certain types of high-potential ventures it simply is not the factor that makes or breaks the majority of business start-up efforts.

4.2. Process characteristics

A central set of variables in research on NE's exploitation process is the *gestation activities* undertaken during the process. The US and Swedish PSED studies included questions concerning a set of more than 20 different activities such as developing a business plan; securing financial resources; deciding on a location for the business; having it formally registered, etc ([61]; [62]). The Norwegian study also included many of those while studies in other countries included much less of this type of information. Some of the gestation activity variables are dichotomous while others have several steps (like not-at-all; initiated; completed), which means a range from zero to over 40 completed behavioral steps can be created on the basis of these variables [45]. The answers were also time stamped by the year and month when the activity was undertaken or initiated, and the set of questions was repeated in each follow-up.

Based on the gestation activities variable set some researchers have made efforts to map out the start-up process itself. An early insight from forerunners of the PSED was that start-up processes can follow almost any sequence – including having first sales before thinking seriously about starting a business[1] ([22]; [112]). Similarly, analysis of US PSED data led Newbert ([102], p. 67) to conclude that there is 'tremendous idiosyncratic variation among respondents' with regard to start-up activities, and Liao and Welsch [91] to propose that firm gestation is a process where developmental stages are hardly identifiable. Focusing solely on characteristics of the process itself, however, Lichtenstein, Carter, Dooley, and Gartner [94] found that compared to discontinued start-up efforts, the continued cases of organizational emergence were characterized by a *slower* pace of start-

---

[1] This sequence is not at all as absurd as it first seems, and probably happens rather frequently for ventures started according to Bhave's [15] 'internally stimulated' logic. This also points at the questionable quality of 'first sale' as outcome variable or marker of the distinction between 'firms in gestation' and 'established business'.

up activities over a longer period of time and, interestingly, a flurry of punctuated activity at the origin or near the conclusion of the effort. On this basis, these authors hold that NEs can improve their chances of success by bringing several start-up activities close to fruition, and then complete them simultaneously, thus creating a 'tipping point' that drives the momentum of their efforts. This 'punctuation' idea is pursued further in a related work where one case was followed concurrently and in-depth during the gestation process [95].

4.3. Process characteristics and outcomes

Lichtenstein's work introduces the topic of how characteristics of the process influence outcomes. While others have provided partial insights into how carrying out specific start-up activities relates to eventual outcomes (e.g., [91]; [103]; [140]) it is a series of papers by Frédéric Delmar and Scott Shane, using a qualified subset of the NEs in the Swedish PSED, that has most intensely penetrated this issue. In Delmar and Shane [54] they explicitly ask whether the order of start-up activities matter. They start with the (average) sequence suggested by 17 Swedish 'expert entrepreneurs' as the normative basis, and analyze the extent to which deviations from this norm punishes NEs with substandard results regarding the obtaining of sales as well as level of sales. They find that the more organizing activities the firm founders undertake the more adverse is the effect of undertaking activities out of the recommended sequence. That is, despite the enormous variations in sequence demonstrated in descriptive research (cf. above) these authors suggest there is indeed a 'best sequence'; a normatively recommendable order of organizing activities. Similarly, in Delmar and Shane [55] the same authors show that undertaking 'legitimating' activities (e.g., business planning; registering a legal entity) early in the process reduces the 'hazard of disbanding', i.e., makes it less likely that the start-up effort will be abandoned. In a third paper they argue that planning should be undertaken before marketing efforts begin and provide analyses that appear to support that proposition [128]. In a fourth paper they use slightly different analyses to support the hypothesis that business planning leads to favorable results in the business creation process [53].[2]

While Delmar and Shane's is the most comprehensive effort so far to sort out, based on NE data, the very complex issue of what is a recommendable process for successfully undertaking a business start-up, their results have not been immediately and unanimously accepted by other researchers who have greater belief in a flexible 'action' as opposed to a 'planning' orientation ([22]; [77], [78]; [119], [120]). And they should not necessarily be accepted, for despite Delmar and Shane's diligent work there are certainly questions that can be validly raised against some of their conclusions. However, when assessing this critique it should be remembered that it is only thanks to Delmar and Shane's work that some of the problems leading to the counter-argumentation were detected; without their work these insights would not have been gained. Some of the issues that may make their conclusions less certain are the following:

- *Causality.* PSED's longitudinal design puts the researcher in a much better position to infer causality than cross-sectional designs do. Yet, some results lend themselves to alternative interpretations. For example, in Delmar and Shane [55] it may well be an unmeasured, higher level of initial commitment (cf. [22]; [35]; [49]) that leads both to the early undertaking of legitimating activities and the later persistence in the process, rather than legitimating activities directly causing survival of the venture. This, of course, is a general problem and in no way particular to the work of Delmar and Shane.

- *Other evidence on the suitability of different types of process.* The main thrust of Delmar and Shane's result is that it propagates a linear, orderly and planned process. As we have already noted, Hills *et al.* [71] and Baltrusaityte *et al.* [12] compared outcomes for NEs following Bhave's [15] presumably more emergent (also in the exploitation phase) 'internally

---

[2] Delmar and Shane interpret the primary role of a business plan as a means of legitimating the venture in the eyes of external parties, which makes it part of the exploitation process. Business planning can alternatively be regarded as part of the discovery process.

stimulated' process with those following the presumably more planned and orderly 'externally stimulated' process, and found no differences. Likewise, Sarasvathy's [121] much recognized reasoning on *effectuation* vs. *causation* processes is relevant here. Her empirical results suggested that expert entrepreneurs show more of the former type of process, which relies less on planning and more on incremental and flexible behavioral steps forward [122]. At the very least one would assume that different types of processes fit better for different types of ventures ([40]; [123]). This relates to the heterogeneity problem discussed below.

- *Other evidence specifically on the effects of business planning.* While Delmar and Shane estimate positive effects of business planning other analyses of the same and similar data set have reported no or very weak effects of planning. For example, Carter *et al.* [22] did not single out planning as a positive factor in their original effort along these lines. In analyses of US PSED data, Newbert [102] found no effect of planning on reaching sales, and neither did Parker and Belghitar [103] in a relatively sophisticated econometric analysis. In a directly comparative analysis Honig and Karlsson [79] found positive effects in the US but not for Swedish NEs of having prepared a written business plan, suggesting the effect may be culture-specific. In alternative analyses of the Swedish PSED data, Honig and Karlsson [78] found only marginal support for business planning enhancing survival, and no support for business planning positively influencing profitability. All in all, Delmar and Shane's interpretations would have been more convincing had their results appeared more robust across samples and model specifications. It should be emphasized, though, that to date no results based on PSED type data seem to support a belief that business planning is harmful. In addition, the particular result that planning (and other legitimating activities) decreased the risk of involuntary but not voluntary termination is an interesting observation that strengthens the Delmar–Shane view on the effect of business planning [52].

- *The nature of the dependent variable.* In part geared in that direction by the logic of their most used analysis method (Event History Analysis), Delmar and Shane's most favored dependent variable contrasts abandoned cases with an 'other' group with all non-abandoned cases. A serious shortcoming of this approach is that the 'other' group will consist of a combination of (a) successful cases; (b) those that unwisely continue what should have been terminated, and (c) those who never put their effort to an 'acid test' and therefore continue to be classified as 'still trying'.[3] The importance of this problem is illustrated by the early finding by Carter *et al.* [22] that the 'up and running' and 'abandoned' cases seemed rather similar (but different from those 'still trying'). These two groups undertook similar activities; the difference seems to be that some arrived at the conclusion that their efforts would lead to a winner while others draw the opposite conclusion.

  Importantly, both may have been right in their assessments (cf. also Diochon *et al.*'s [57] findings about those who abandoned often doing so voluntarily). If business start-ups are regarded as experiments with uncertain outcomes, the only failed cases are the experiments that never lead to a conclusive answer.[4] Abandoned cases, by contrast, may in many instances be regarded as experiments that successfully determined at reasonable cost that what initially seemed to be a profitable business opportunity probably was not. This shows that abandoned vs. not-yet-abandoned – especially if interpreted as failed vs. (more) successful – is not a suitable dependent variable in research on nascent entrepreneurs. Therefore, normative conclusions like 'Our results demonstrate that entrepreneurs should complete business plans before talking to customers or initiate marketing and promotion' ([128], p. 783) should not be drawn on the basis of such analyses. For example, it may

---

[3] It should be noted, however, that Delmar and Shane made an effort to reduce the problem of 'eternal still trying cases' by only accepting into their analysis cases that were initiated within approximately nine months prior to the original interview.

[4] However, and making this issue even more complicated, Parker and Belghitar [103] point out that there are theoretical reasons to believe that waiting can sometimes be valuable.

be the case that some of the planners who continue do so unwisely as victims of well known psychological phenomena such as 'escalation of commitment' [98] or 'failure to use negative information' [48]. It should be noted here that Delmar and Shane's [54] results concerning deviations from the 'experts' recommended process are not subject to this caveat.

- *The nature and heterogeneity of the sample.* The PSED-type studies to date have aimed at obtaining nationally representative samples. This is one of the strengths of the research, but also one of its weaknesses. One of the things researchers involved in this research have learnt is that a simple, random sample of business start-ups will be dominated by rather mundane, low uncertainty and low potential efforts in mature industries. Therefore, if Delmar and Shane [54] have indeed distilled a 'one best process' out of their data it is to that kind of business start-up this result is generalizable. Further, a simple random sample of business start-ups will by necessity be a very heterogeneous sample along many dimensions. As has been demonstrated in works reviewed below, there is reason to analyze sub-groups separately rather than assuming that the sample is homogenous enough to yield meaningful results without sub-divisions.[5]

- *The nature of the operationalization.* Finally, it should be noted that limitations of the PSED data may make the process appear more directional and linear than it actually is because once a gestation activity is reported as completed no further information is collected on later elaboration or modification on that specific dimension.

In summary, Delmar and Shane's work on the venture start-up process is a good example of growth of scholarly knowledge in this domain. If one is willing to accept their results the series of papers by Delmar and Shane has made major strides forward in our understanding

---

[5] It is perhaps superfluous to point out that sub-dividing the sample leads to the problem of not having enough cases to analyse, and the number of cases was a factor that Delmar and Shane simply had to accept at the outset of their work.

of the NE exploitation process. For those who remain doubtful, their work has made major strides forward for our ability to identify and articulate what precisely has to be done in future research in order to arrive at results one can have confidence in. One of the obvious steps forward is to look for differences across types of NEs and types of venture start-ups. This work, which has already begun, is what will be reviewed in the next sub-section.

4.4. Process characteristics and outcomes for various subgroups of NEs

Observing the heterogeneity problem, several researchers have analyzed sub-samples by different 'types' of NEs or ventures. For example, in his dissertation work Samuelsson ([119]; [120]) first demonstrated that two subgroups representing innovative vs. imitative (the latter alternatively being labeled 'reproducing' or 'equilibrium opportunities') start-ups can be distinguished empirically. The former group is much less numerous than the latter. He then went on to demonstrate that different factors explain outcomes for the two groups. For example, with respect to making progress in the process, education level had a positive effect for innovative ventures but a negative effect for imitative ventures (possibly reflecting better 'other alternatives' or a higher prevalence of businesses 'on the side' for the more highly educated). Just as for Davidsson and Honig [45], the analyses also indicate differential effects at different stages of the process. For example, 'instrumental social capital' is relatively more important for imitative ventures, and its importance increases over time, whereas 'emotional social capital' has an effect only initially and only for innovative ventures. Unlike Lichtenstein *et al.* [94] and Alsos and Kolvereid [7], Samuelsson [120] also found that those who undertake more activities per time unit are more likely to succeed, leading him to promote a 'doer' approach to venture creation.

Further, Samuelsson's ([119]; [120]) results demonstrate that variables included in the PSED research can explain a fair amount of the outcome variance for the minority of innovative ventures but an almost embarrassingly small share of the outcome variance for imitative ventures. This indicates that either the design is based on implicit or explicit theories that are not very good at explaining the latter phenomenon, or the imitative group is still too heterogeneous for any strong generalities to shine through.

Starting from a dynamic capabilities framework and using the US PSED data, Newbert [102] made a similar distinction among low, moderate and high tech start-ups. Echoing Samuelsson's findings, the amount of variance explained is highest for the high tech, and lowest for the low tech group. Newbert [102] found differences in the explanatory models for the different groups but although he made a worthy attempt to put forward theoretical rationales for some of them, many differences regrettably appear rather haphazard, reflecting that this line of research still has a long way to go before fully satisfactory ways of measuring, explaining and interpreting patterns in the exploitation process have been developed.

In a similar vein Liao and Welsch [92] tested a set of hypotheses concerning the exploitation of 'tech' vs. 'non-tech' nascent ventures. First, they found support for the hypothesis that the gestation period is longer for technology-based ventures. This is another result that signals that great care must be taken with selection of dependent variable and interpretation of 'success' in this type of research. The fact that the process takes longer does not preclude that the venture will eventually be more financially successful. Second, their results confirm that technology-based venture start-ups undertake a greater number of start-up activities. Again, this is a group difference with method implications. At reaching the same specific number of completed activities (and perhaps even the same activities) one venture may effectively be up and running while the other still has a long way to go. The result also confirmed sub-hypotheses that the level of activity was more intense for technology-based ventures concerning activities relating to legitimacy, planning and marketing, but not for resource transformation. Finally, Liao and Welsch [92] did not find the systematic sequencing differences that they expected between the two categories.

Analyzing Norwegian data, Alsos and Kolvereid [7] compared types of NEs rather than types of ventures. More specifically, they contrasted the exploitation process for novice, serial, and parallel founders, i.e., those who do it for the first time compared with those who have done it before and those who engage in a start-up alongside already running one or more firms (cf. [151]). Not very surprisingly, both categories of 'habitual' entrepreneurs turned out more likely to invest own money and to hire employees. Neither is it surprising that the parallel founders devote less time to the start-up. Other results are less obvious. It turns out that parallel founders are more likely to form a team; make use of government funding, and engage in sales promotion activities. A common pattern here seems to be to make other people and their resources work for you. Despite the slower pace of the process parallel founders are also more likely to generate income at an early stage and eventually to get the venture up and running, which are perhaps indications that these are people who know how to play the 'entrepreneurial game'. The sequencing of activities appeared similar for the groups, but the serial founders were more likely to devote full time and complete a number of activities early on. Interestingly, the results indicate that while the parallel founders show several signs of being 'professional business founders', the serial founders do not appear on average to do much better than the novices. This leads to yet another important insight for theory and method: one reason for becoming 'serial' founder is failure at previous attempts, and in some cases these failures indicate low skill. This suggests that a sample of 'habitual entrepreneurs' – and perhaps serial ones in particular – will be 'contaminated' by a sub-set of founders who habitually fail (cf. [89]). This suggests that researchers may be better off starting from a theory-based criterion of 'expertise' rather than mere empirical evidence of prior experience, when contrasting more and less accomplished entrepreneurs (cf. [70]).

The Norwegian team has also compared the exploitation process for male and female NEs [8]. These results will be reviewed in the 'Some Particular Themes' section.

4.5. Conclusion

The exploitation process is a phenomenon for which concurrent, longitudinal research on nascent entrepreneurs can truly make unique contributions. At this point, it is probably a fair assessment to say that what has been done so far represents a very promising start of that work. As regards factors associated with more or less favorable outcomes the research community is beginning to build an ability to distinguish among factors that increase (a) the probability of entering into nascent entrepreneurship; (b) the propensity to persist in such endeavors, and (c) the likelihood of success. As regards process characteristics, the time-stamped 'gestation activities' have turned out to be one of the most useful and versatile aspects of the PSED design, making possible many truly new insights.

However, the research conducted so far has also revealed that the exploitation process is a far more complex phenomenon to successfully penetrate than the researchers involved may have imagined at the outset. Consequently, considerable work remains to be done. Theoretical development and deeper empirical investigation are needed in order to correctly interpret some of the initial findings. For example, it would quite possibly be a mistake to accept at face value that financial capital and human capital dimensions such as education level and managerial experience are unimportant for successful exploitation of venture ideas just because these variables fail to consistently yield significant, positive effects in regression analyses. Underlying processes that may conceal positive effects of education and experience are that the better qualified may have a higher frequency of starting sideline businesses and/or be more likely to terminate the process because of more attractive employment opportunities, and/or apply higher standards for what constitutes a level of performance high enough to make a continued effort worthwhile [66]. As regards financial capital the case may be that individuals start whatever businesses available means allow them to start, so that the effect shows in terms of type of business started and later survival rates, rather than in very early outcome variables such as making progress in the process and achieving first sales. In this context it is worth considering Geroski's [65] observation that high barriers to survival rather than high barriers to entry seem to characterize many industries. On the other hand, Grilo and Thurik's [69] failure to find any effect of their finance variable across all levels of engagement in entrepreneurial activities (including having given up a start-up effort and being an ex-owner-manager of a business) rather supports the notion that for most business start-ups the finance dimension truly is not the most crucial one at any stage of development.

As regards process characteristics there is a need for stronger conceptualizations regarding what the various types of gestation activities represent, as well as some level of agreement across researchers on that issue. The above review has also highlighted the heterogeneity problem, which leaves work to do regarding how to best define and locate the most relevant sub-samples, or else deal with the heterogeneity in the analysis. Not least has the work to date revealed that researchers need to take greater care in the selection and interpretation of the dependent variable. For example, there have been repeated indications that achieving sales may not always signal reaching anything near completion of the process; that abandonment does not necessarily represent a 'worse' outcome than continuation, and that a longer process is not always an inferior one.

5

Some Particular Themes

The US PSED paid special attention to issues of *gender* and *ethnicity* via over sampling and – to some extent – inclusion of questions emanating from a special interest in entrepreneurship among women and ethnical minorities ([21]; [68]). The *team characteristics* section of the questionnaire was also well developed [4]. In addition, several manuscripts about NEs have focused on their *growth aspirations* [80]. These themes are what will be reviewed in this section.

5.1. Characteristics and dynamics of new venture teams

In a descriptive analysis, Aldrich *et al.* [4] note that a majority on NEs work in teams. After weighing to correct for the women and minority over sampling the proportions in the US data are 48% solo NEs and 52% team NEs. For Sweden, an even higher proportion of team NEs has been reported, viz. 56–58% ([45]; [55]). While it demonstrates that team entrepreneurship is a common phenomenon this result does *not* mean that a majority of nascent *ventures* are started by teams. This brings us to a fundamental and largely unresolved issue with the PSED design: is it a sample of individuals or a sample of ventures? If the latter, team start-ups become over sampled with the approach used because there are more individuals (and households) who represent a team start-up than a solo start up [42]. So far, surprisingly few researchers have explicitly addressed this issue.

Aldrich *et al.* [4] further report that most teams, 74%, have only two members. The proportions then fall monotonically, with 17, 7 and 5%, respectively, having three, four, and five or more members. Touching upon issues for the following two sub-sections, they further note that as many as 64% of the teams are mixed gender and 86% single ethnicity. Importantly, the reason for the frequent occurrence of mixed gender teams is that 53% of the team NEs join forces with their spouse or romantic partner. Another 18% have non-spouse family members as team mates, while 15% team up with business associates. All in all this demonstrates the importance for an empirical researcher to get the basics right. First, team start-ups are very frequent, so the implicit assumption in early entrepreneurship research studies that one person equals one venture is clearly a flawed idea leading to flawed research design. Second, however, the ubiquity of team NEs does *not* mean a very high frequency of high-powered, well-balanced teams that have been formed solely for competence-based and/or economic-rational reasons. Rather, the high proportion of team NEs is a consequence of a combination of over sampling (in a sense) of team based ventures and the high incidence of spouses, other romantic partners and family members venturing into business together.

This is further demonstrated in Ruef, Aldrich, and Carter [117]. This work investigates US PSED teams more deeply in terms of the extent to which *functionality, homophily, status expectations, network constraints*, and *ecological constraints* determine team composition. The results clearly point out that homophily and network constraints imposed by strong (i.e., family) ties are the most powerful forces behind team formation. In plain English this means that other than the gender mix resulting from real or *de facto* spouses venturing together, teams are mostly made up by people who are similar in terms of gender, ethnicity and occupational background. Little support was found for teams being formed with the purpose of having different team members cover different functional specializations. A particularly surprising result was a tendency *away* from occupational diversity in larger teams.

Ruef *et al.* [117] did not investigate how team composition relates to outcomes. Their contribution lies rather in the sophistication of the analysis, separating 'romantic' teams from the others and applying an analysis technique that forces one to compare with the relevant base rates, leading to a realistic empirical description of the phenomenon of team entrepreneurship. As has been noted already this phenomenon is dominated by inter-individual relationships quite different from the entrepreneurial team in the typical entrepreneurship textbook (e.g., [137]). Based on the latter, one would suspect Ruef *et al.*'s descriptive results to be normatively questionable. Aldrich, Carter, Ruef, and Kim [5] have started the investigation of how NE team composition relates to outcomes. While they could confirm that team start-ups were significantly more likely than solo efforts to become 'up and running' firms, they found no indication that gender homophily made any difference with respect to this outcome. The effect of ethnic homophily was difficult to discern because differences between ethnic groups overshadowed effects of having an ethnically homogenous team. It should be noted that similarity and diversity regarding educational and occupational experiences were not investigated.

Kim and Aldrich [85] looked instead at the effect of changes in the team over time on business outcomes. They found that teams with stable ownership structures were more likely to be operating rather than still being in an active start-up phase. Further, for teams with more than two members the change in team composition was low both for firms achieving operating status and those remaining in an active start-up phase. They also found operating start-ups to be less likely to have changes in racial composition. In all, the results lead the authors to speculate that team stability is conducive of achieving operating status.

Combining analysis of Swedish data with those of a US sample of young firms, Chandler, Honig, and Wiklund [28] also investigated effects of team (in)stability. Their research question concerned whether team size and heterogeneity affect the occurrence of changes in team composition, and whether the latter in turn influence performance, operationalized as reaching profitability. Based on the Swedish PSED data they found that larger teams were more likely to add new members, but not more likely to drop members. These results were reversed, however, for their American sample. Further, teams that added members were less likely to have reached profitability. The authors interpret this as adding members being a disruptive event that often has dysfunctional consequences. However, the result may alternatively be interpreted as (a) the venture being in trouble already, causing *both* the addition of a new member (supposedly as an intended remedy to the problem) and the sub-standard performance, or (b) that they belong to a category of more complex start-ups, requiring both more diverse skills (hence the adding of team members) and longer time to reach profitability.

5.2. Gender

The main findings from NE research about gender issues are easy to summarize. First, there is a very consistent under representation of women among nascent entrepreneurs. Second, once in the process there are few differences between men and women concerning how they go about organizing the new venture, and what outcomes they accomplish to reach.

As regards female participation in nascent entrepreneurship the most recent GEM data suggest that across countries, there are about twice as many male as female NEs; i.e., women make up about one third of all NEs [1]. The gender divide is particularly wide in southern Europe while in the US the gap is much smaller. Verheul and Thurik [142] show that essentially the same factors explain male and female participation across countries. Further, while they found no good predictor directly related to the female share of NEs, the by-gender analysis suggests that the female participation rate in the work force is one major explanation why the relative under representation of women in entrepreneurship varies by country. The observation in early GEM reports that the female-to-male ratio tends to be higher in countries with high over all levels of business start-up activity is in line with this explanation [111]. Other institutional factors may aggravate the problem. For example, Davidsson and Henreksson [44] discuss the reason why Sweden – which has very high general work force participation among women – has a larger sex difference in NE prevalence than, e.g., the US. They argue that institutional arrangements – especially regulation of health care and education as well as tax levels that render many personal and household services non-marketable – have systematically hampered women's ability to exploit their educational and vocational assets through starting and running independent businesses.

The results obtained by Davidsson and Honig [45] are an example of the typical pattern. While their analysis contrasting characteristics of NEs and the comparison groups yields a highly significant result for sex, none of the analyses concerning making progress or reaching financial outcomes indicated strong or reliable effects attributable to the sex of the founder(s). Using various outcome variables, Diochon *et al.* [57] and Parker and Belghitar [103] have confirmed the absence of gender effects on outcomes for Canadian and US data. Newbert [102] further demonstrated that this holds true both overall and for groups of NEs at different levels of technological sophistication. Further, Matthews and Human [97] found no gender difference in growth expectations in the US PSED, while Schoett and Bager [126] found higher growth aspirations among men in Danish data, and Cassar [25] found that the relationship between start-up motives (independence and financial gain) and growth aspirations was stronger for female than for male NEs.

Alsos and Ljunggren [8], who focused particularly on process differences between male and female entrepreneurs, found some process differences but no differences in outcomes. Specifically, they found a marginally lower percentage of women reporting having prepared a business plan. Further, women NEs were more likely to apply for (subsidized) government funding help, but given application there was no sex difference in receiving such assistance. Women NEs were substantially less likely to have hired employees. One out of three indicators of speed or intensity of the process, *viz.* the average number of months between the initiations of activities, yielded a marginally significant lower score for women (see Davidsson and Honig [45], who found a similar, weak tendency). Importantly, however, most of the differences identified by Alsos and Ljunggren [8] were small, and they were not associated with outcome differences.

All in all, the results so far suggest there is every reason not to exaggerate gender differences in nascent entrepreneurship. In essence the results indicate no differences in outcomes; some rather small differences in process, and a marked and consistent difference in entry. It can be questioned even for the latter difference whether it represents an effect specifically related to entrepreneurship. For example, Reynolds [104] demonstrated that in a (truly) hierarchical, multivariate analysis the rather clear bivariate difference by sex has a tendency to disappear, suggesting that more fundamental, institutional factors that create differences in, e.g., education and work experience are at work, rather than the female under representation reflecting an entrepreneurship-specific, 'innate' difference by sex. If there is a 'pure' gender difference it may have to do with entrepreneurship generally being 'male gendered' [3], making it less considered by women, or seem less attractive to them. Within the confines of nascent entrepreneurship research, Wagner [146] has suggested that an entrepreneurship specific gender difference may reside in the relative fear of failure. He cites general and entrepreneurship specific literature to back up the notion that women tend to perceive more risk, and also to be more risk averse. However, this gender by fear-of-failure interaction hypothesis does not hold up in Arenius and Minniti's [10] analysis of cross-national GEM data. On the contrary, in their analysis of US GEM data Köllinger and Minitti [88] found a significant negative effect of 'fear of failure' on NE propensity only for white men.

5.3. Ethnicity

Other than the team results discussed above, the issues of ethnicity, minorities and immigrants has so far not been much analyzed in the nascent entrepreneurship research. This is despite this dimension being singled out for over sampling in the US PSED study [68]. One early indication, however, shows the importance of the research approach and the tremendous sociological implications of the results. This is that the pattern for African Americans (and possibly Hispanics) seems to be the opposite of that for women. That is, while other data suggest African Americans are under represented among the self-employed, the

PSED data show they are at least equally represented, and more likely markedly over represented among NEs ([67]; [68]; [84]). Analysis of US GEM data confirms this result [88]. Thus, while female under representation is related to never trying in the first place, under representation of some minorities seems related either to problems getting start-up efforts to an operational stage, or to differential survival rates (cf. [88]). This suggests radically different strategies for policies towards overcoming the problems of under representation in the respective groups.

Some studies, like Delmar and Davidsson [50], report over representation of immigrants among NEs, while Kim *et al.* [84] do not find such an effect in the US PSED. This, however, adds nothing new to the literature. It has been well established for a long time in the entrepreneurship literature that some immigrant groups are over represented while others are under represented among independent entrepreneurs [130]. The reasons for this are less investigated. A remaining task is therefore to disentangle the extent to which over representation in certain immigrant groups is contingent on (a) discrimination in the work market for employment; (b) entrepreneurial cultural heritage from the specific group of origin, and (c) self-selection of entrepreneurial individuals among those who show the initiative to break up from their old country and start anew elsewhere.

5.4. Growth aspirations

Previous research has provided indirect as well as direct evidence that entrepreneurs' growth motivation predicts a meaningful amount of variance in actual, subsequent growth ([36]; [56]; [99]; [154]), making the study of NEs growth aspirations a somewhat more meaningful exercise than it otherwise would have been. The main results so far on this topic can be summarized in a couple of sentences: NEs' future expectations for their businesses are typically very modest. Yet, they are probably higher than the average start-up manages to realize. For example, Delmar and Davidsson [49] report for Sweden that out of 405 NEs, 306 and 208 of them expected to have only 0–1 employees after one and five years, respectively. Further, the internal non-response was high for five year projections, suggesting many of them had not even thought about what size of firm they were trying to create. Human and Matthews [80] show that aspirations are typically low for US-based NEs as well. For example, the median expected revenue after five years is a mere USD 100 000, and on a dichotomous attitudinal item 78% say they prefer to keep the firm at a manageable size rather than growing it as large as possible.

Schoett and Bager [126] combined NE data with data for groups of established firms that are young and mature, respectively. This is how they arrive at the conclusion that despite the above, NEs actually exaggerate their expansion prospects. A complicating factor regarding the generalizability of this finding is that for some reason the Danish NE's growth aspirations do not appear quite as modest to begin with as in some other countries. For example, 30% of their NEs expect to reach and employment size of 10–99 employees within five years. At any rate, Schoett and Bager [126] interpret the higher aspirations of the NEs relative to the other groups as showing that either do those with higher aspirations abandon the start-ups at a higher rate (cf. Gimeno *et al.*'s [66] results concerning differential thresholds for continuing), or the NEs learn to adapt to more realistic goals. Referring to Brown and Kirchhoff [20], Carter *et al.* [22], and Shane [127], Schoett and Bager argue that both effects have been identified before. Regarding the learning and adaptation hypothesis, psychological and economic theories suggested by Lewin, Dembo, Festinger, and Sears [90] and Jovanovic [81] are also worth mentioning in this context. As regards PSED-based empirical results Diochon *et al.* [57] confirm that growth-orientated NEs are more likely to disengage from the start-up. Analyzing a German PSED pilot study Welter [149] made the same interpretation based on cross-sectional differences between NEs and established firm owner-managers. Her observations of the different determinants of growth aspirations for NEs and established entrepreneurs are actually very interesting as they suggest that the underlying reason may be that higher levels of human capital, i.e., more education and experience, may lead to more realistic goals and therefore higher levels of goal completion. This would reconcile some instances of surprisingly weak effects for HC variables on projective performance measures.

When it comes to explaining variance in NEs growth aspirations the short story is that this is difficult to do. Delmar and Davidsson [49] tried a variety of explanatory models based on different theories and sets of independent variables, and then combined the best predictors in a final model. Their interpretation was that a set of indicators likely to reflect the NE's level of *commitment* (incorporation as legal form; expectation that business would provide main income; number of gestation activities initiated/completed; growth as explicit goal) had some predictive ability. Given the results just discussed concerning growth-orientated NEs greater propensity to disengage the label 'commitment' should perhaps be exchanged for 'ambition' – which also points at a certain circularity in the result. Other than this, Delmar and Davidsson's [49] main conclusion is that the ability to predict the (projected) future development of business start-ups is very limited. US results reported by Matthews and Human [97] and Matthews, Ford, and Human [96] essentially boil down to the same conclusion. For Denmark, across their three samples Schoett and Bager [126] found some support for five out of eight hypotheses about dispositions that drive growth aspirations. However, only two hypotheses, viz. higher growth aspirations for men and for those with higher self-reported entrepreneurial competence, gained support in the NE sample. Moreover, the gender difference is not supported by Matthews and Human [97] and with one remaining significant difference out or eight – and a percept-percept based one at that (cf. [33]) – the pattern for Danish NEs comes close to statistical expectation based on stochastic variation. Cassar [25] was able to establish that goals of financial success was the most important determinant of growth aspirations among US NEs, which he holds challenges earlier reports that non-economic concerns are relatively more important determinants of business owner-managers' growth willingness [153]. Liao and Welsch's [93] demonstration of how different forms of social capital (and financial, but not human capital) influence growth aspirations represent perhaps the theoretically most meaningful findings to date in this area, although some of their operationalizations of SC may be a stretch of that theoretical concept.

In summary, the analyses of NEs growth aspirations have helped create a realistic image of the modesty of the typical new venture start-up. There are also interesting indications in the material that some start-ups have high aspirations for the wrong reasons (incompetence; over-optimism) while others have modest aspirations for the right reasons (realism). It is further quite clear that those with higher aspirations are more likely to abandon the start-up. This, again, demonstrates the care that must be taken in this type of research regarding selection of the dependent variable and interpretation of results relating to that variable. While attempts to explain variation in growth aspirations have generally only enjoyed very moderate success, Liao and Welsch's [93] results emphasize the importance of social capital (or a supportive environment) in forming ambitious goals for the start-up.

6

The Bigger Picture

On an aggregate level, the most important outcome of the GEM and PSED research is perhaps its portrayal of the enormity of this phenomenon. The GEM research has yielded estimates that about *500 million* people were simultaneously involved in nascent or recent entrepreneurial activity, out of a base rate of six billion [106]. Including indicators also of past involvement in business start-ups the research approach has demonstrated that even in a country like Sweden – which has comparatively low NE prevalence rates ([44]; [107]) – almost 30% of the adult population has had direct experience from involvement in independent start-ups at some point in their lives, and in the US that proportion is closer to 40% [50]. Against this background, it is easy to agree that what this research has achieved is that '. . . the results have transformed the perspectives of policymakers and scholars alike. Never again will entrepreneurship be seen as a peripheral activity unrelated to economic adaptation and change . . .' ([106], p. 226).

Importantly, however, far from all nascent entrepreneurs pursue business start-ups with high potential and/or for positive reasons. For example, in 2003 some 27% of the NEs characterize their efforts as necessity-driven rather than opportunity-driven. This is probably still a low estimate. Further, only one NE in 33 expects their venture to have significant innovative impact [107]. Variance across countries in the relative prevalence of such subgroups suggests that a raw count of NE prevalence captures partly different phenomena in different countries.

The GEM research has revealed enormous cross-country variation in total NE prevalence rates, with anything from 1 to 40% of the adult population being directly involved in an on-going business start-up effort at a given point in time. Among structurally similar, industrial countries the range of variation is considerably narrower – and the phenomenon under investigation possibly more comparable – but it is surely not an unimportant finding that countries like Japan, France and the Netherlands consistently show much lower prevalence rates than Anglo-Saxon countries ([1]; [107]; [108]; [109]; [110]; [111]).

Investigating the causes and effects of such variation is the primary target for scholarly research based on the GEM data. Towards that end, a first research conference dedicated solely to analyses of GEM data was held in Berlin in April 2004. A selection of papers from that conference appears in a special issue of the journal *Small Business Economics* (Vol. 24, No. 3). Although other sources will also be used, this set of articles will form the backbone of the remainder of this section. It should be noted that in GEM based research the prevalence of NEs is often combined with the prevalence of recently started firms in the so called 'TEA Index.'

Within-country regional effects on NE prevalence have been reported by, e.g., Delmar and Davidsson [50] for Sweden and by Wagner and Sternberg [148] for Germany. For the US different studies have arrived at significant [104] and non-significant [84] differences among Census Regions. However, other types of research have been more informative regarding regional differences in entrepreneurial activity within countries (e.g., [11]; [113]). Davidsson and Henreksson [44] used PSED and GEM data to establish that Sweden has a comparatively low NE prevalence rate. They explain this by carefully examining a set of institutional arrangements and showing that they are systematically biased against the birth (and growth) of new, independent firms. However, their analysis included no systematic comparison of institutional arrangements across countries, leaving room for alternative explanations for the low NE prevalence rate in Sweden.

Salimath, Cullen, and Parboteeah [118] make an interesting attempt to analyze the influence of cultural and institutional variation by compiling such data from other sources and relating them to GEM prevalence data across 22 countries. At this point, however, their results appear too tentative to allow any confident interpretations. More convincing is a very interesting analysis of 36 GEM countries by Wennekers, Stel, Thurik, and Reynolds [150], who likewise include supplementary data from other sources. These authors attempt to make sense of the U-shaped relationship between level of economic development and NE activity, which emerges from the GEM data (Verheul and Thurik [142] also include this U-shaped relationship in their analysis but employ a different main focus). Wennekers *et al.* [150] show that it is variance in opportunity-based entrepreneurship that is the driver of the non-linearity. That is, necessity-based entrepreneurship decreases with the level of economic development. The important conclusion from this research is that it suggests different policy strategies for countries on different levels of development. For the most advanced countries improving incentive structures for start-ups (and the commercialization of scientific findings) are the most promising policy alternatives, according to these authors. Developing nations may be better off pursuing the exploitation of scale economies; foreign direct investment, and improved management education.

In a related paper Stel, Carree, and Thurik [135] explicitly make NE activity the independent variable, and relate it to GDP growth across 36 GEM countries. They also include a Growth Competitiveness Index, compiled from other sources, as independent variable so as not to over ascribe explanatory power to independent start-up activity. They do find relationships, but in accordance with the results obtained by Wennekers *et al.* [150] a significant, positive effect is found only for rich countries and not for transition economies or developing countries. One of the analyses instead suggests the effect for poorer countries is significantly negative. In line with these differential results Acs and Varga [2] may have been wise to delimit their analysis to the nine European Union countries that participated in GEM. For these countries they found significant but not very strong effects of (agglomeration and) entrepreneurial activity on technological change. Finally, Wong, Ho, and Autio [155] related different versions of the TEA index to GDP growth per worker. Their results show miniscule regression effects for overall TEA as well as for opportunity- and necessity-based version of the index. Their newly computed 'high-growth potential TEA' did, however, come out with a statistically significant effect of meaningful magnitude. Consequently, these authors argue that it is not just any business start-up activity but specifically that with higher potential that drives economic development. It should be emphasized that such a finding is not trivial or self-evident. Other research has suggested that because of their vast numbers the more modest start-ups may actually sum up to greater aggregate effects [47]. Wong *et al.* [155] also included data from other sources, viz. patenting statistics, in their analysis so as not to over ascribe results to new venture creation.

In all, the aggregate level analysis have helped map out the nature and scope of nascent (and recent) entrepreneurial activity across countries worldwide. This has forced a development towards greater sensitivity to 'types' of nascent entrepreneurs and emerging new ventures. Scholars have also demonstrated that for aggregate level analysis the GEM data can be very useful for cross-national comparison because other statistics on start-up activity may not exist or are less comparable due to different data collection procedures. The GEM data can therefore lead to unique new insights, especially if combined with data from other sources on other country characteristics. The attempts to use GEM data for micro level analysis have been relatively less successful, as the number of variables and sophistication of measurement fall short of what is needed for meaningful analysis on that level of detail.

7

Developments So Far

7.1. An atheoretical research endeavor?

One of the criticisms of research on nascent entrepreneurship is that it has not been sufficiently driven by theoretical insights and concerns, gearing researchers towards exercises in empirical fact finding that may not make the results travel through space or stand the test of time (cf. [40], p. 33). To some extent such criticism is no doubt valid. To a considerable extent, however, it builds on limited insights into the nature and history of this research. As regards GEM, it is first and foremost a policy research project aimed at addressing issues of immediate social interest and relevance in the participating countries. As such, it has been enormously successful ([43]; [106]). Its design builds on a crude conceptual framework that reflects a combination of economic theory; previous, tentative empirical generalizations, and a dose of common sense. It has never aspired to contribute to any particular theoretical research frontier. This is not to deny, of course, that the quality of the policy advice emanating from the project would likely benefit from stronger theoretical input. It should also be noted, however, that in many participating countries little or no academic entrepreneurship research was undertaken before. Therefore, the GEM study can act as the catalyst that directs the right human and financial resources to academic research in this area, similar to the igniting effect of the Bolton Report in the UK and David Birch's classical study on job creation in the US ([16]; [18]).

As regards PSED, a large number of theoretical perspectives contributed to the design of the study [64]. In one sense the problem is rather that the study aims to incorporate so many theoretical perspectives that no single theory could be allotted the questionnaire space needed for a more comprehensive test. The financial reality behind this is that a rather large team, involving some 30 academic institutions, had to join forces in order to make the study feasible at all [63]. Needless to say, with so many interests sharing the same limited space the questionnaires would not allow comprehensive testing of any one theory. Further, there is little doubt that some sections of the questionnaires are purely exploratory and phenomenon-driven rather than theoretically anchored. However, even this may be defensible. It must be remembered that the core target of the PSED research is the *process of emergence;* i.e., a combination of two issues on which few extant theories in any discipline do a particularly good job.

7.2. Increased theoretical sophistication

There has undoubtedly been a development towards increased theoretical sophistication over time. In the earlier works (e.g., [7]; [8]; [22]; [49], [50]; [104]; [149]) the word 'theory' or any of its derivatives is rarely mentioned, and specific hypotheses are not developed or tested. The section between 'Introduction' and 'Method' is typically labeled 'Literature Review' or 'Previous Research.' The titles of these works also reveal that they are largely explorative, fact-finding exercises driven by a curiosity about the empirical phenomenon of firm emergence.

Around the year 2000 there seems to be a turning point where the research starts to address specific hypotheses (e.g., [51]; [119]) although concepts clearly pointing at specific theories do not appear in the main title. In more recent works (e.g., [45]; [55]; [78]; [84]; [93]; [102]; [117]) there is typically a section called 'Theory'; 'Theoretical Development'; 'Theoretical Framework' or 'Conceptual Development.' Further, hypotheses are developed and formally tested, and theoretical concept like 'Human Capital'; 'Legitimacy'; 'Institution', and 'Strong Ties' typically appear in the main title. In fact, the PSED research has been far more theory-driven than this review may indicate, as space limitations prohibit the reporting in full of the theoretical vantage points and interpretations with which the various contributors associate their results. To give a few brief examples, Davidsson and Honig [45] base their hypotheses and interpretations on theories of human and (different forms of) social capital. Delmar and Shane [54] draw upon institutional theory as well as two strands of evolutionary theory. Their other papers are structured in a similar way. Kim *et al.* [84] and Liao and Welsch [93] are similar examples based on the US PSED, while Newbert [102] uses the dynamic capabilities framework in developing his hypotheses.

A particularly fine example, in this author's opinion, is Honig and Karlsson's [78] work on business planning. Based on institutional theory, their analyses tell a rather interesting, coherent and somewhat provocative story about business planning as an activity pursued because of mimetic and coercive institutional pressures rather than because it helps produce favorable results (cf. [46]). In their analysis, the relationship to business outcomes is weak or non-existent. Another very fine example of theory-driven NE research that has reached prestigious publication is Ruef *et al.*'s [117] work on team composition, which was described above in the 'Teams' sub-section.

Researchers have also demonstrated the suitability of using GEM data for theory-testing purposes. This includes, e.g., theories concerning the effects of agglomeration ([2]; [115]) as well as exogenous and endogenous growth theory ([2]; [155]). Other theoretical perspectives have also been employed ([118]; [136]).

In summary, there has been a laudable re-direction towards more explicit and sophisticated conceptualization in NE research over time. This is not to suggest that this development is without problems. One problem is that different researchers select whatever indicators are available in these publicly (or at least widely) available data sets in order to operationalize concepts they were not originally intended to measure, i.e., a threat to validity. While the upside of this is the versatility of the data sets a more ideal process would have the same theories guide design, data collection and analysis. It may also be questioned whether knowledge of the investigated phenomenon has advanced far enough for this branch of research to turn wholeheartedly to theory-testing. However, at this stage of development it may be argued that exploration based on longitudinal cases, or interplay between qualitative and quantitative exploration, may be more commendable that further exploration of quantitative data alone ([94]; [95]; [132]).

7.3. Increased methodological sophistication

There has also been considerable development towards increased methodological sophistication over time within this line of research. As regards *sample construction*, the original criterion for the fundamental question of 'who is a nascent entrepreneur?' was an affirmative answer to the question 'Are you, alone or with others, now trying to start a new business?'[1] In the final US PSED design the qualifier was added in the screening interview that the respondent expected to be a (part) owner of the venture. The GEM studies have subsequently added two additional qualifiers in order to determine whether cases may be under- or over-qualified as NEs (i.e., inactive or already to be considered operational firms). Using PSED type data, various researchers have used responses concerning gestation activities in the ensuing phone interview to arrive at a more precisely defined set of eligible cases. For example, Delmar and Davidsson [49] required respondents to have completed at least two 'gestation activities' in order to qualify, and considered cases as already started if (a) money had been invested *and* (b) a legal entity had been formed *and* (c) income had been made from the business. Delmar and Shane ([52], [53], [54], [55]) used a slightly different set of criteria. Most importantly, they excluded cases that were initiated more than approximately nine months prior to the initial interview, thus reducing problems of retrospection and low intensity efforts that should perhaps not be regarded serious start-up attempts. Shaver, Carter, Gartner, and Reynolds [131] thoroughly discuss the

---

[1] The interview screens also for 'nascent intrapreneurs'. However, as explained in the introduction, this review is delimited to analyses concerning nascent entrepreneurs.

problem of exactly determining NE status in a paper that regrettable has not been published in full length. The issue is also dealt with in the PSED Handbook (e.g., [23]). While there is no consensus – and perhaps there cannot be – on who or what should and should not be regarded a valid case it is probably safe to suggest that there is now more widespread insight that this is an issue that the researcher cannot take lightly.

As regards using NE prevalence as indicator of level of entrepreneurial activity the GEM research has progressed from using the overall NE rate to including it as one of several indicators, and refining the analysis by distinguishing between necessity- and opportunity-driven NEs; innovative vs. imitative start-ups, and separating those with high growth potential from all others ([1]; [107]; [108]; [109]; [110]; [111]). In 2003 a new index was added to gauge innovative intentions among established firms [107]. Thus, the research has gradually made it possible to use the data for various definitions of 'entrepreneurial activity'. Analyses provided by Wennekers *et al.* [150] and Wong *et al.* [155] have demonstrated how critically important these distinctions are.

Regarding other *operationalization* issues researchers have shown considerable creativity in using a combination of PSED items to create new variables that are more robust or reflect other concepts than the original items can capture on their own. This goes not least for the gestation activities ([21]; [62]), which have proven particularly useful and versatile. They have been used as single items (e.g., [128]) and as aggregate indices (e.g., [45]); as independent (e.g., [92]) as well as dependent [120] or control variables [128]. They have also been used for determining whether cases are under- or over-qualified as NEs [131] and for re-organizing the data set ([55]; cf. below). Further, using the time stamping of the activities researchers have computed new variables like *duration* (time elapsed since first gestation activity), *recency* (time since most recent activity) and *efficiency* (average time between activities) ([49]; cf. [7] and [22]). Samuelsson's [120] comprehensive indices for 'instrumental' and 'emotional' social capital are other examples of how items have been combined to create new and hopefully more robust measures.

As regards *organization of the data set*, level of analysis problems occur at re-interviewing points when the respondent has left a team that is otherwise still working on the start-up as well as when the respondent is still an NE but working on a completely different start-up. In order to deal satisfactorily with such cases the Swedish PSED team created two versions of the data set, one of which follows 'surviving' individuals and the other following surviving ventures. Data collection and inclusion of valid cases were organized accordingly. Another problem with the PSED data is that the cases have been active for different duration of time when they are first caught by the screening interview. In their series of papers, Delmar and Shane ([52], [53], [54], [55]) have dealt with this by excluding cases that have already been active for a long time and by re-organizing the data set according to the time of first activity rather than time of first interview.

It is perhaps with regards to *analysis methods* that the greatest development has been visible. For analysis of categorical outcomes an early and useful step towards increased sophistication and relevance was Reynolds' [104] application of CHAID (Chi-square based Automatic Interaction Detection) for analyzing NE prevalence in different socio-demographic sub-groups; a practice later picked up by Delmar and Davidsson [50]. The approach communicates much more efficiently than most other methods, findings regarding in what sectors of society entrepreneurial activity is high and low. Otherwise the categorical analyses (such as NE vs. non-NE or current status of the start-up effort in 2–4 categories) have moved from bivariate frequency comparisons ([7]; [50]) and more exploratory multivariate techniques such as one-way ANOVA and discriminant analysis [22] to the more causally orientated logistic regression technique ([45]; [102]) and further to rather sophisticated multinomial logit modeling with Heckman correction for non-random attrition ([103]; cf. also [53]). In order to overcome the problem of bias because of uneven group sizes – a situation that often occurs in entrepreneurship research; cf. Reynolds [104]–Wagner ([144], [146]) pioneered the use of Rare Events Logistical Regression [86] for analysis of NE data.

As regards sequencing, where Carter *et al.* [22] and Alsos and Kolvereid [7] used little in the way of formal techniques Liao and

Welsch ([91], [92]) more recently used new and advanced graphical, node-linking techniques within the Clementine® package. Other examples of application of 'non-standard' methods as tools for reaching farther include Samuelsson's ([119]; [120]) use of Latent Class Analysis for substantiating the existence of more and less innovative subgroups; Ruef *et al.*'s [117] use of Structural Event Analysis; van Gelderen *et al.*'s [140] application of PRINCALS (a factor analytic technique that can handle 'ordinal' data) and Lichtenstein's [95] sophisticated techniques for analysis of longitudinal case studies. Further, analysts have moved on from exclusively examining linear, additive models to including interaction effects ([28]; [144]) and non-linearity [135] – as well as demonstrating the critical importance of such more ambitious modeling for our understanding of the phenomena under scrutiny. The previously discussed analyses of more homogenous subgroups can also be mentioned in the same category ([7]; [93]; [102]; [119], [120]).

Two developments in particular have been introduced that allow making more full use of the longitudinal nature of the PSED data. One is Delmar and Shane's reorganization of the data set into monthly spells and application of Event History Analysis for relating process characteristics to outcomes ([52], [53], [54], [55]; [128]). Even though great care must be taken with the dependent variable this technique is likely to prove a fruitful tool for further research into the venture gestation process. The second example is Samuelsson's ([119]; [120]) introduction of LGM (*Longitudinal Growth Modeling*; see [100]; [101]). As this technique is designed to predict both initial state and development over time it also addresses the problem of the cases being first captured at different stages in the gestation process. Further, as it is designed for the use of a continuous variable (e.g., accumulation of gestation activities) it is an excellent complement to Event History Analysis, which is designed for binary outcomes. The latter technique, on the other hand, is better at handling the attrition problem. Hence, a combination of both may be needed in order to arrive at a more correct portrayal of the true process dynamics [120].

In summary, considerable development is evident on the method side in nascent entrepreneurship research. Thanks to these developments, researchers who now begin to analyze – or design the collection of – this type of data start from a much better foundation than what was available when the PSED project started for real some ten years ago.

8

Further Development Needs

In this author's opinion, the above review has proven the PSED-GEM approach to research on nascent entrepreneurs a workable, meaningful and very promising way of gaining new and deeper insights into new venture creation. While the above has shown that considerable development has occurred in this young strand of research its very youth warrants it should come as no surprise that further improvements are possible. Based on the above review and other insights into this line of research, this section will be dedicated to such further possibilities for improvements. These will be presented in the form of propositions. In line with the opening of this section, the first proposition is:

> *Proposition 1: The PSED 'early catch and then follow up' approach is essentially sound and should remain a standard tool in empirical entrepreneurship research.*

However, although the current methodology has worked quite well there may be reasons to revise even this fundamental aspect of the design. Essentially, the current methodology allows the respondents to decide whether they should report themselves as NEs or not. This works fine if the criterion is allowing enough to include all cases that are intended to be eligible, and researcher-controlled criteria can be used subsequently to narrow down the sample to include only valid cases. There are signs, however, that under reporting of cases intended to be valid does occur. For example, in Germany and Ireland there have been issues of suspected underreporting when the standard PSED-GEM question is asked, possibly because individuals in 'craft industries' and independent professionals do not necessarily see what they are setting up as a 'business' (C. O'Gorman, F. Roche, and F. Welter, personal communication). In addition, ventures that are started out of first solving a problem for oneself rather than a wish to go into self-employment, i.e., Bhave's [15] 'internally stimulated' process, may advance quite far and encompass several completed 'gestation activities' before the individual(s) involved think of what they are doing as 'starting a business'. This may lead to under reporting of such cases, or confounding of early catch with fast completion if this category on average has proceeded further when first included in the sample. Moreover, the researcher may want to include 'social/non-profit' entrepreneurship as well, or postpone judgment regarding the distinction between such cases and 'regular' entrepreneurship. For these reasons:

> *Proposition 2: The screening for a valid sample of NEs should start with the broadest self-perceived definition of NE that is practically possible, and rely on researcher-controlled criteria for narrowing down from there to the sample finally judged eligible.*

The fact that NEs are relatively rare makes the PSED-GEM procedure for locating a large, nationally representative sample relatively costly. The reward, if the process is successful, is statistical representativeness and hence comparability. The downside is that the sample will be very heterogeneous and dominated by imitative, low-potential ventures. While the GEM experience is that country differences are relatively stable over the years and correlations of different temporal and concurrent indicators of entrepreneurial activity are generally high ([1]; [107]), there are also cases where individual countries show rather erratic patterns, which appear not to be unrelated to changes of supplier of the interviewing services ([73], [74]). In combination with the Germany-Ireland issues discussed above this shows the importance of exactness in execution of harmonized procedures. As regards heterogeneity, the GEM researchers have successfully addressed this problem by assessing different types of nascent entrepreneurship. For PSED type research, which aims at more theory-driven and fine-grained analysis, the heterogeneity of the sample and the dominance of low potential ventures are more serious problems. Further, social science is not the same as opinion polls, and theories are not constructed by democratic vote. Generalizations are aimed to ultimately refer to theoretical categories, not to a specific empirical population in a particular country at a particular time. Hence, the fact that a particular type of venture is more common than another does not automatically make it theoretically more important, so that one should let it dominate the results ([46], Ch. 5). It is therefore not a given that a simple random sample is the most suitable for investigating theory-driven, micro level research questions concerning nascent entrepreneurship and firm emergence. Some pre-stratification based on education or profession/vocation of respondents may be possible in some countries, but in general the prospects for probabilistic sampling of more narrowly defined categories of NEs are very limited. In order to get, for example, sufficient numbers of high-tech and/or high-potential ventures run by teams assembled for competence reasons it may therefore be necessary to use other sampling mechanisms than probability sampling.

Proposition 3: For GEM type, aggregate level research questions statistical *representativeness, ensured through probability sampling; culturally adapted harmonization; high response rates, and weighing in relation to population data, are essential features. Heterogeneity problems can be satisfactorily dealt with via a small number of classification variables and – possibly – somewhat larger samples.*

Proposition 4: For PSED type process research purposes theoretical representativeness is the more important issue. Therefore, the sampling should ensure sufficient representation of theoretically interesting types of ventures, even at the cost of sacrificing probability sampling.

The non-random sampling of NEs from disadvantaged groups can, e.g., be captured among applicants to governmental assistance programs whereas higher potential start-ups at early stages can be identified via business incubators and business angel networks. If researchers resort to non-probability sampling of 'interesting' ventures it would be highly advantageous to do so as an addendum to a 'conventional' PSED study, as there will always be a need for relevant yardsticks to compare with (cf. below).

Related to the heterogeneity problem it is being increasingly emphasized that issues of *fit* and *interdependence* are relatively more important than universal factors that influence all cases equally ([38], [40]; [127]; [129]). In the above review this has turned up in the form of radically different sub-sample results and critically important interaction effects.

Proposition 5: Researchers conducting this type of research need to pay more attention to the heterogeneity of NE samples by (a) sampling more narrowly; (b) applying theories that predict and explain particular forms of heterogeneity; (c) applying sub-sample analysis, and (d) modeling and evaluating interaction effects (i.e., moderator variables).

Another problem that the review has revealed is the issue of level of analysis. Is the sample a sample of nascent entrepreneurs; of firms in gestation, or perhaps of cases illustrating 'the individual-opportunity nexus' [129]? While all three are possible, it is this author's conviction that the design is better suited for analysis on the (emerging) venture level rather than the individual level. For reasons elaborated elsewhere, relating individual characteristics to the fate of a single venture over a limited period of time does not do justice to psychological theory nor to the real importance of person-related variables [41]. Another problem with the individual level is the confusion between 'nascent' and 'novice'. It is really the venture that is 'nascent'; PSED research demonstrates that a significant share of individuals involved already run other businesses or previously have done so. With teams the issue is different because the team is usually uniquely associated with one and only one venture.

Proposition 6: PSED type research can have the individual, the team, the venture, or the specific venture – individual(s) combination as the focal unit. Importantly, however, the choice of theory, informant(s), operationalizations, and criteria for regarding cases as (still) valid should consistently reflect this choice of level of analysis.

Proposition 7: PSED type research is best suited for venture and/or team levels of analysis.

For team level research, the analyses by Aldrich and co-workers have demonstrated that such work should start by separating spouse teams (incl. de facto) from other teams. As regards the venture level, influential entrepreneurship scholars have noted that entrepreneurship has tended to be 'one-legged' in its detailed examination of personal characteristics of the individuals involved whereas very little attention has been paid to characteristics of the emerging venture itself, or 'the opportunity' as Shane and Venkataraman [129] denote it. Hence, future research in this area would benefit from paying more attention to characteristics of the emerging venture and how it evolves over time from a crude idea to an operational business model.

The review has further revealed that while the PSED-GEM procedure, when successful, yields a probabilistically representative sample of nascent entrepreneurs on a given date, it does in a certain sense lead to over sampling of team start-ups and of processes of longer duration (cf. [42]). Further, the procedure does not produce a 'clean' cohort; the cases eventually included will not have been initiated at the exact same point in time and hence some of them will be close to completion while others just barely fulfill the minimum criteria for being regarded a valid case. The most obvious error that can arise from this is that factors that lead to rather late (self-identification and) reporting of NE status may mistakenly be interpreted as success factors because such cases may complete the process more quickly (cf. Proposition 2).

Proposition 8: Researchers conducting this type of research should be aware of the potential over sampling of teams and 'long' processes and apply remedies to these biases if they are deemed important considering the specific research questions being pursued.

Proposition 9: Researchers conducting this type of research should be aware that cases are not equally far advanced when first captured and apply satisfactory remedies to this problem.

As indicated above, this author does not believe exact statistical representation relative to a particular empirical population to be the most critical issue, and sometimes weighing of the data to reflect such a population may actually conceal theoretically important findings. However, when correction of team and length-of-process is deemed important this can be accomplished with the help of weighing based on data from the surveys concerning the number of members in the team and the time elapsed since the first gestation activities compared with the average time in the sample. For the problem highlighted in Proposition 9 it is difficult to conceive of a process orientated analysis situation where this would *not* be a problem. There are different ways in which it can be addressed with different levels of sophistication. First, already established design elements of assessing and time stamping all relevant gestation activities should be retained. Second, the time since first activities and/or the number of activities already completed can be used as control variables in hierarchical, multivariate analysis. Third, the data set can be re-arranged based on the timing of the first activity/activities, so that cases are aligned according to this criterion. Due to the great variance in process sequencing ([22]; [91]; [102]) it is probably not possible or advisable to align them according to a *particular* activity. Finally, an analysis method such as LGM that explicitly models variance in initial state can be used ([119], [120]).

A very important issue for future research will be the selection and interpretation of the dependent variable. The review has shown that first sales can come early in the process rather than marking the articulation into operating status; that 'abandonment' is not necessarily a worse outcome than continuation; that different ventures may need to complete different numbers of activities in order to achieve operating status, and that their (successful) gestation process may require different amounts of time. This will render careless or mindless application of *any* available outcome variable highly dubious. Moreover, in PSED type research so far the status of the venture in terms of 'abandoned', 'dormant', still active' and 'up and running' has so far relied on the respondent's perception of the meaning of these classifications, which is highly unsatisfactory.

> *Proposition 10: In continued work on NEs/the venture gestation process it is imperative that the greatest care be taken in the selection and interpretation of the dependent variable. In order to yield meaningful, credible results the DV must be theoretically relevant and validly operationalized.*

While the problem of relevant performance measurement is not unique to this line of research (cf. [30]) and while no perfect solutions readily present themselves, there are a number of steps forward that researchers can take. As regards categorical status of the venture this should more ideally be based on as researcher-defined criteria as possible. Perhaps a combination of status on a pre-defined set of the 'gestation activities' would present a good solution, especially if these were assessed in a refined manner, allowing more dynamism to be captured. Second, in analyses of categorical outcomes more than two categories may have to be included – and the analysis method accordingly chosen. If the analysis method dictates two outcomes the pairwise contrasting of several categories may be better than lumping together cases that threaten to represent theoretically very different phenomena in a single 'other' category. When abandonment is used as an outcome criterion the interpretation can be improved if the analysis distinguishes between 'voluntary' and 'non-voluntary' abandonment, or between cases terminated with and without significant financial loss. Further, the assessment of financial outcomes such as sales and profitability can be refined as regards the magnitude and regularity of these phenomena. When completion of gestation activities is used the 'not relevant for this venture' responses can be used more than they apparently have been so far. This would allow computation of new variables such as 'percent of relevant activities completed' and 'number of relevant activities yet to be completed.' Such variables would help better align and compare venture gestation processes requiring different degrees of complexity. Finally, allowing a longer time separation between cause and effect may reduce the tendency to discriminate against cases that take longer to reach (possibly greater) eventual success, and to give the true effect of the explanatory variables enough chance to shine through (cf. [14]; [152]). It should also be noted that for analyses on the individual and team levels completely different dependent variables than 'venture performance' may be more theoretically relevant [41].

A problem that comes with longitudinal research, and which most of the NE literature is surprisingly silent about, is the issue of attrition. It is as if researchers – including the undersigned – shrugged their shoulders and were content that the problem was not worse (because the general experience has been that continued participation among eligible cases is rather high). However, as some of the methodologically sophisticated researchers in this area have noted, attrition is a problem that must be addressed in order not to arrive at biased results ([54]; [103]).

Proposition 11: In future research on nascent entrepreneurship researchers should explicitly address the problem of attrition.

There are various ways in which this can be done. One, which has already been employed, is to work hard to keep up levels of continued respondent cooperation in the data collection phase. Another is to apply researcher-controlled criteria for defining cases as 'abandoned' or 'up and running' and thus not to drop such cases too lightly from continued data collection, or to change the contents of interviews on a questionable basis. In the analysis phase partial remedies include applying analysis methods that are designed to deal with attrition [128] or correcting for non-random attrition [103]. When one's main method requires complete data the alternatives at hand are to perform supplementary analyses in order to get some sense for the severity of the problem [120] or to apply sophisticated methods for data imputation ([58]; [124]).

While the review has demonstrated increased sophistication of conceptualization and use of theory in this line of research, this is another area where further developments are needed. Among many possible examples, those of Honig and Karlsson [78] and Ruef *et al.* [117] show that careful application of strong theory to extant NE data can lead to new, provocative or unexpected insights, and make wonders for the meaning of the empirical relationships that are investigated. Conversely, the above discussed 'contamination' of habitual entrepreneurs with habitual failure-creators demonstrates that the research would benefit from using a theoretically defined notion of 'expertise' – rather than just experience – as the vantage point. The tendency of researchers to use whatever variables are available and regard them as indicators of their favorite theoretical concepts demonstrates the risk of not having the same theoretical perspective govern the entire research process. The result may well be that research is portrayed as more theory-driven than actually is the case, as well as invalid theoretical interpretations being superimposed upon given empirical relationships (cf. [156]).

However, the process of venture emergence is a phenomenon which few extant theories explicitly address. Therefore, it is also important not to let the confines of extant theory restrict what can be discovered about the phenomenon. Hence, researchers may find it necessary to combine and adapt existing theories in order to make useful tools out of them, or even to develop new theory. Before uncritically adopting existing theories 'as is' these are some of the questions worth asking for a researcher investigating venture creation (cf. [46], p. 51): Does the theory acknowledge uncertainty and heterogeneity? Can it be applied to the phenomenon of emergence? Can it illuminate process issues? Does it apply to the preferred level of analysis? And is it compatible with the type of outcomes the researcher is interested in?

Where extant theory does not suffice a combination of qualitative and quantitative exploration appears a sound way forward ([94]; [95]), provided the end result be strong concepts on a high enough level of abstraction. When qualitative work is done in isolation there is risk for getting lost in idiosyncratic detail; when quantitative analysis is used without close-up familiarity with the phenomenon the corresponding risk is arms-length misinterpretation of the true nature of relationships. Qualitative data could potentially put necessary flesh on the bones regarding the role and effects of business planning as well as on such results as, e.g., the weak effects of human and financial capital on making progress as nascent entrepreneur. Quantitative data can determine the strength and generality of observations and interpretations originating from qualitative analysis.

Proposition 12: Continued research in this area will benefit more from letting existing theory govern the analysis than from solely using curiosity about the phenomenon for guidance.

Proposition 13: Continued research in this area will benefit even more from letting the same theory/theories guide design, operationalization, data collection and analysis, so that unsound, post hoc pairing of empirical items (and results) with theories can be avoided.

Proposition 14: For theoretical development where extant theory does not suffice a combination of longitudinal case studies and conventional PSED type data may prove a fruitful way forward.

As regards analysis methods the above review has shown that there has already been considerable development. Researchers who enter this field can get a good start by investigating what 'non-standard' methods have already been applied in NE research. Some of this development has been lucky coincidence.[1] With more systematic search via discussions with statisticians and researchers outside their own and the closest neighboring fields, researchers are likely to encounter new techniques that are better suited for the task of analyzing heterogeneous, emerging phenomena longitudinally than is the package of central-tendency focused and variance-explaining methods that normal Ph.D. training in Management provides one with.

---

[1] For example, Samuelsson ([119]; [120]) more or less stumbled over and started to learn a novel method – LGM – early in the process and well before realizing that this method was more or less perfectly suited for the research problem he was going to focus on.

Proposition 15: Researchers in this field should continue the search for and application of 'alternative' analysis techniques that can make better use of PSED type data.

As a note on interpretation, Carter *et al.*'s [24] findings about career reasons highlight the constant need for yardsticks in this type of research, i.e., the need for a relevant basis of comparison. Another such reminder that many results cannot be meaningfully interpreted in isolation is that while Human and Matthews [80] find approximately an 80 to 20 preference for keeping the firm at a manageable size over growing it as large as possible, Schoett and Bager [126] arrive at almost the reverse for a similar looking item, although expressed more weakly as preference for 'expansion' vs. 'stability'. The fact that subtle differences in wording can alter results in a dramatic fashion has previously been demonstrated by, e.g., Kahneman and Tversky [82] in their famous research on Prospect Theory. The lesson is clear; while meaningful interpretations can be made concerning differences between groups that are exposed to the exact same question, and between points in time for repeated measures on the same sample, results like these have very uncertain absolute meaning.

Proposition 16: Researchers working with this kind of data should avoid making 'absolute' interpretations and always make sure a relevant yardstick for comparison exists.

Finally, the review was suggestive also for the use of GEM data for scholarly purposes:

Proposition 17: For scholarly purposes, GEM data are best used for aggregate level analysis and in combination with data from other sources. For micro level analysis they have very limited potential.

9

Conclusion

This review has attempted to show that the PSED/GEM approach to capture on-going start-up efforts and studying their concurrent development longitudinally is a basically sound, workable approach that has opened up a new and very promising avenue for entrepreneurship research. While many interesting results have already been reported and while considerable improvements on both the method and theory sides of research have been made, there is still room and need for further improvements. In the preceding section an attempt was made to give as precise as possible guidance – albeit certainly not entirely complete – regarding how this research can be further developed. While no researcher or project should be expected to make all these improvements at once it is hoped that the above assessment will facilitate progress in this area of research. From the perspective of a new entrant to the field it is still close to virgin ground and the interesting opportunities and challenges to take on are innumerable.

References

[1] Z. J. Acs, P. Arenius, M. Hay, and M. Minniti, *GEM 2004 Executive Report*, Babson College/London Business School, Boston and London, 2005.

[2] Z. J. Acs and A. Varga, "Entrepreneurship, agglomeration and technological change," *Small Business Economics*, vol. 24, pp. 323–334, 2005.

[3] H. J. Ahl, *The Making of the Female Entrepreneur*, Doctoral dissertation, Jönköping International Business School, Jönköping, 2002.

[4] H. E. Aldrich, N. M. Carter, and M. Ruef, "Teams," In: *Handbook of Entrepreneurial Dynamics: The Process of Business Creation*, Gartner, W. B., Shaver, K. G., Carter, N. M., and Reynolds, P. D., Sage, Thousand Oakes, pp. 299–310, 2004.

[5] H. E. Aldrich, N. M. Carter, M. Ruef, and P. H. Kim, "Hampered by homophily? The effects of team composition on the success of nascent entrepreneurs' organizing efforts (Summary)," In: *Frontiers of Entrepreneurship Research 2003*, Bygrave, W. D. *et al.*, Babson College, Wellesley, MA, 2003.

[6] H. E. Aldrich and P. H. Kim, "Against all odds: The impact of financial, human and cultural capital on becoming a nascent entrepreneur," Paper presented at the conference: Nascent Entrepreneurship: The Hidden Potential (CD), Durham, 2005.

[7] G. A. Alsos and L. Kolvereid, "The business gestation process of novice, serial and parallel business founders," *Entrepreneurship Theory and Practice*, vol. 22, no. 4, pp. 101–114, 1998.

[8] G. A. Alsos and E. C. Ljunggren, "Does the business start-up process differ by gender? A longitudinal study of nascent entrepreneurs," In: *Frontiers of Entrepreneurship Research 1998*, Reynolds, P. D. *et al.*, Babson College, Wellesley, MA, 1998.

[9] P. Arenius and D. De Clerck, "A network-based approach on opportunity recognition," *Small Business Economics*, vol. 24, pp. 249–265, 2005.

[10] P. Arenius and M. Minniti, "Perceptual variables and nascent entrepreneurship," *Small Business Economics*, vol. 24, pp. 233–247, 2005.

[11] C. Armington and Z. J. Acs, "The determinants of regional variation in new firm formation," *Regional Studies*, vol. 36, no. 1, pp. 33–45, 2002.

[12] J. Baltrusaityte, Z. J. Acs, and G. E. Hills, "Opportunity recognition processes and new venture failure: Examination of the PSED data," Paper presented at the Babson College/Kauffman Foundation Entrepreneurship Research Conference, Wellesley, MA, 2005.

[13] A. Bandura, "Self-efficacy mechanism in human agency," *American Psychologist*, vol. 37, pp. 122–147, 1982.

[14] J. R. Baum and E. A. Locke, "The relationship of entrepreneurial traits, skill, and motivation to subsequent venture growth," *Journal of Applied Psychology*, vol. 89, no. 4, pp. 587–598, 2004.

[15] M. P. Bhave, "A process model of entrepreneurial venture creation," *Journal of Business Venturing*, vol. 9, pp. 223–242, 1994.

[16] D. L. Birch, *Job Creation in America: How the Smallest Companies Put the Most People to Work*, The Free Press, New York, 1987.

[17] S. Birley and P. Westhead, "A taxonomy of business start-up reasons and their impact on firm growth and size," *Journal of Business Venturing*, vol. 9, pp. 7–31, 1994.

[18] J. E. Bolton, *Small Firms. Report of the Committee of Inquiry on Small Firms*, Her Majesty's Stationery Office, London, 1971.

[19] R. H. Brockhaus, "The psychology of the entrepreneur," In: *Encyclopedia of Entrepreneurship*, Kent, C. A., Sexton, D. L., and Vesper, K. H., Prentice Hall, Englewood Cliffs, NJ, pp. 39–71, 1982.

[20] T. E. Brown and B. A. Kirchhoff, "The effects of resource availability and entrepreneurial orientation on firm growth," In: *Frontiers of Entrepreneurship Research 1997*, Reynolds, P. D., Bygrave, W. D., Carter, N. M., Davidsson, P., Gartner, W. B., Mason, C. M., and McDougall, P. P., Babson College, Wellesley, MA, pp. 375–389, 1997.

[21] N. M. Carter and C. Brush, "Gender," In: *Handbook of Entrepreneurial Dynamics: The Process of Business Creation*, Gartner, W. B., Shaver, K. G., Carter, N. M., and Reynolds, P. D., Sage, Thousand Oaks, pp. 12–25, 2004.

[22] N. M. Carter, W. B. Gartner, and P. D. Reynolds, "Exploring start-up event sequences," *Journal of Business Venturing*, vol. 11, pp. 151–166, 1996.

[23] N. M. Carter, W. B. Gartner, and P. D. Reynolds, "Firm founding," In: *Handbook of Entrepreneurial Dynamics: The Process of Business Creation*, Gartner, W. B., Shaver, K. G., Carter, N. M., and Reynolds, P. D., Sage, Thousand Oaks, pp. 311–323, 2004.

[24] N. M. Carter, W. B. Gartner, K. G. Shaver, and E. J. Gatewood, "The career reasons of nascent entrepreneurs," *Journal of Business Venturing*, vol. 18, pp. 13–29, 2003.

[25] G. Cassar, "Entrepreneur motivation, growth preferences and intended venture growth (Summary)," Paper presented at the Babson College/Kauffman Foundation Entrepreneurship Research Conference, Strathclyde, Scotland, 2004.

[26] G. N. Chandler, J. Dahlqvist, and P. Davidsson, "Opportunity recognition processes: A taxonomic classification and outcome implications," In: *Frontiers of Entrepreneurship Research*, Bygrave, W. D. *et al.*, Babson College, Wellesley, MA, 2002.

[27] G. N. Chandler, J. Dahlqvist, and P. Davidsson, "Opportunity recognition processes: A taxonomy and longitudinal outcomes," *Academy of Management Meeting*. Seattle, 2003.

[28] G. N. Chandler, B. Honig, and J. Wiklund, "Antecedents, moderators and performance consequences of membership change in new venture teams," *Journal of Business Venturing*, vol. 20, pp. 705–725, 2005.

[29] C. C. Chen, P. G. Greene, and A. Crick, "Does entrepreneurial self-efficacy distinguish entrepreneurs from managers?," *Journal of Business Venturing*, vol. 13, pp. 295–316, 1998.

[30] A. C. Cooper, "Challenges in predicting new firm performance," *Journal of Business Venturing*, vol. 8, pp. 241–253, 1993.

[31] A. C. Cooper and F. J. Gimeno-Gascon, "Entrepreneurs, processes of founding and new firm performance," In: *The State of the Art in Entrepreneurship*, Sexton, D. and Kasarda, J., PWS Publishing Co., Boston, MA, 1992.

[32] A. C. Cooper, F. J. Gimeno-Gascon, and C. Y. Woo, "Initial human and financial capital as predictors of new venture performance," *Journal of Business Venturing*, vol. 9, no. 5, pp. 371–395, 1994.

[33] S. M. Crampton and J. A. Wagner, "Percept-percept inflation in microorganizational research: An investigation of prevalence and effect," *Journal of Applied Psychology*, vol. 79, no. 1, pp. 67–76, 1994.

[34] B. Crosa, H. A. Aldrich, and L. A. Keister, "Is there a wealth effect? Financial and human capital determinants of business start-ups," In: *Frontiers of Entrepreneurship Research 2002*, Bygrave, W. D. *et al.*, Babson College, Wellesley, MA, 2002.

[35] J. Dahlqvist, P. Davidsson, and J. Wiklund, "Initial conditions as predictors of new venture performance: A replication and extension of the Cooper *et al.* study," *Enterprise and Innovation Management Studies*, vol. 1, no. 1, pp. 1–17, 2000.

[36] P. Davidsson, "Continued entrepreneurship: Ability, need, and opportunity as determinants of small firm growth," *Journal of Business Venturing*, vol. 6, no. 6, pp. 405–429, 1991.

[37] P. Davidsson, *Determinants of Entrepreneurial Intentions*, Working Paper 1995:1, Jönköping International Business School, Jönköping, 1995.

[38] P. Davidsson, *Researching Entrepreneurship*, Springer, New York, 2004.

[39] P. Davidsson, "Role models and perceived social support," In: *Handbook of Entrepreneurial Dynamics: The Process of Business Creation*, Gartner, W. B., Shaver, K. G., Carter, N. M., and Reynolds, P. D., Sage, Thousand Oakes, pp. 179–185, 2004.

[40] P. Davidsson, "The entrepreneurial process: Lessons for entrepreneurship education," *International Journal of Entrepreneurship Education*, vol. 3, pp. TBD, 2005.

[41] P. Davidsson, "Method challenges and opportunities in the psychological study of entrepreneurship," In: *The Psychology of Entrepreneurship*, Baum, J. R., Frese, M., and Baron, R. A., Ch. 13, Erlbaum, Mahway, NJ, 2005.

[42] P. Davidsson, "Method issues in the study of venture start-up processes," In: *Entrepreneurship Research in Europe: Outcomes and Perspectives*, Fayolle, A., Kyrö, P., and Ulijn, J., Edward Edgar, Cheltenham, UK, pp. 35–54, 2005.

[43] P. Davidsson, "Paul Davidson Reynolds: Entrepreneurship research innovator, coordinator and disseminator," *Small Business Economics*, vol. 24, no. 4, pp. 351–358, 2005.

[44] P. Davidsson and M. Henreksson, "Institutional determinants of the prevalence of start-ups and high-growth firms: Evidence from Sweden," *Small Business Economics*, vol. 19, no. 2, pp. 81–104, 2002.

[45] P. Davidsson and B. Honig, "The role of social and human capital among nascent entrepreneurs," *Journal of Business Venturing*, vol. 18, no. 3, pp. 301–331, 2003.

[46] P. Davidsson, E. Hunter, and M. Klofsten, "The discovery process: External influences on refinement of the venture idea," In: *Frontiers of Entrepreneurship Research 2004*, Zahra, S. *et al.*, Babson College, Wellesley, MA, 2004.

[47] P. Davidsson, L. Lindmark, and C. Olofsson, "Smallness, newness and regional development," *Swedish Journal of Agricultural Research*, vol. 28, no. 1, pp. 57–71, 1998.

[48] P. Davidsson and R. Wahlund, "A note on the failure to use negative information," *Journal of Economic Psychology*, vol. 13, pp. 343–353, 1992.

[49] F. Delmar and P. Davidsson, "Firm size expectations of nascent entrepreneurs," In: *Frontiers of Entrepreneurship Research 1999*, Reynolds, P. D., Bygrave, W. D., Manigart, S., Mason, C., Meyer, G. D., Sapienza, H. J., and Shaver, K. G., vol. 19, Babson College, Wellesley, MA, pp. 90–104, 1999.

[50] F. Delmar and P. Davidsson, "Where do they come from? Prevalence and characteristics of nascent entrepreneurs," *Entrepreneurship and Regional Development*, vol. 12, pp. 1–23, 2000.

[51] F. Delmar and J. Gunnarsson, "How do self-employed parents of nascent entrepreneurs contribute?," In: *Frontiers of Entrepreneurship Research 2000*, Reynolds, P. D. *et al.*, Babson College, Wellesley, MA, 2000.

[52] F. Delmar and S. Shane, "What founders do: A longitudinal study of the start-up process," In: *Frontiers of Entrepreneurship Research 2002*, Bygrave, W. D. *et al.*, , Wellesley, MA, pp. 632–645, 2002.

[53] F. Delmar and S. Shane, "Does business planning facilitate the development of new ventures?," *Strategic Management Journal*, vol. 24, pp. 1165–1185, 2003.

[54] F. Delmar and S. Shane, "Does the order of organizing activities matter for new venture performance?," In: *Frontiers of Entrepreneurship 2003*, Reynolds, P. D. *et al.*, Babson College, Wellesley, MA, 2003.

[55] F. Delmar and S. Shane, "Legitimating first: Organizing activities and the survival of new ventures," *Journal of Business Venturing*, vol. 19, pp. 385–410, 2004.

[56] F. Delmar and J. Wiklund, "The effect of the entrepreneur's growth motivation on subsequent growth: A longitudinal study," Paper presented at the Academy of Management Meeting, Seattle, 2003.

[57] M. Diochon, M. Menzies, and Y. Gasse, "Insights into the dynamics of Canadian nascent entrepreneurs' start-up efforts and the role individual factors play in the process," Paper presented at the 20th Annual CCSBE Conference, Victoria, 2003.

[58] M. Fichman and J. N. Cummings, "Multiple imputation for missing data: Making the most of what you know," *Organizational Research Methods*, vol. 6, no. 3, pp. 282–308, 2003.

[59] W. B. Gartner, "'Who is an Entrepreneur?' is the wrong question," *American Small Business Journal*, vol. 12, no. 4, pp. 11–31, 1988.

[60] W. B. Gartner, "Words lead to deeds: Towards an organizational emergence vocabulary," *Journal of Business Venturing*, vol. 8, pp. 231–239, 1993.

[61] W. B. Gartner and N. M. Carter, "Entrepreneurial behavior and firm organizing processes," In: *Handbook of Entrepreneurship Research*, Acs, Z. J. and Audretsch, D. B., Kluwer, Dordrecht, NL, pp. 195–221, 2003.

[62] W. B. Gartner, N. M. Carter, and P. D. Reynolds, "Business start-up activities," In: *Handbook of Entrepreneurial Dynamics: The Process of Business Creation*, Gartner, W. B., Shaver, K. G., Carter, N. M., and Reynolds, P. D., Sage, Thousand Oakes, pp. 285–298, 2004.

[63] W. B. Gartner, K. G. Shaver, N. M. Carter, and P. D. Reynolds, "Foreword," In: *Handbook of Entrepreneurial Dynamics: The Process of Business Creation*, Gartner, W. B., Shaver, K. G., Carter, N. M., and Reynolds, P. D., Sage, Thousand Oakes, pp. ix–xxiii, 2004.

[64] W. B. Gartner, K. G. Shaver, N. M. Carter, and P. D. Reynolds, *Handbook of Entrepreneurial Dynamics: The Process of Business Creation*, Sage, Thousand Oaks, CA, 2004.

[65] P. A. Geroski, "What do we know about entry?," *International Journal of Industrial Organization*, vol. 13, pp. 421–440, 1995.

[66] J. Gimeno, T. B. Folta, A. C. Cooper, and C. Y. Woo, "Survival of the fittest? Entrepreneurial human capital and the persistence of underperforming firms," *Administrative Science Quarterly*, vol. 42, pp. 750–783, 1997.

[67] P. G. Greene, N. M. Carter, and P. D. Reynolds, "Minority entrepreneurship: Trends and explanations," In: *New Movements in Entrepreneurship*, Steyaert, C. and Hjorth, D., vol. 239–257, Elgar, Cheltenham, 2003.

[68] P. G. Greene and M. M. Owen, "Race and ethnicity," In: *Handbook of Entrepreneurial Dynamics: The Process of Business Creation*, Gartner, W. B., Shaver, K. G., Carter, N. M., and Reynolds, P. D., Sage, Thousand Oakes, pp. 26–38, 2004.

[69] I. Grilo and A. R. Thurik, "Determinants of entrepreneurial engagement levels in Europe and the US," Paper presented at the conference: Nascent Entrepreneurship: The Hidden Potential (CD), Durham, 2005.

[70] V. Gustafsson, *Entrepreneurial Decision-Making*, Doctoral dissertation, Jönköping International Business School, Jönköping, 2004.

[71] G. E. Hills, G. T. Lumpkin, and J. Baltrusaityte, "Opportunity recognition: Examining search formality, search processes and the impact on firm founding (Summary)," Paper presented at the Babson College/Kauffman Foundation Entrepreneurship Research Conference, Strathclyde, Scotland, 2004.

[72] G. E. Hills and R. P. Singh, "Opportunity recognition," In: *Handbook of Entrepreneurial Dynamics: The Process of Business Creation*, Gartner, W. B., Shaver, K. G., Carter, N. M., and Reynolds, P. D., Sage, Thousand Oakes, pp. 259–272, 2004.

[73] K. Hindle and S. Rushworth, *Sensis GEM Australia, 2002*, Swinburne University, Melbourne, Australia, 2002.

[74] K. Hindle and S. Rushworth, *Westpac GEM Australia. A Study of Australian Entrepreneurship in 2003*, Westpac Corp. and Swinburne University, Melbourne, Australia, 2003.

[75] B. Honig, "Learning strategies and resources for nascent entrepreneurs and intrapreneurs," *Entrepreneurship Theory and Practice*, vol. 24, no. Fall, pp. 21–35, 2001.

[76] B. Honig, P. Davidsson, and T. Karlsson, "Learning strategies of nascent entrepreneurs," *Journal of Competence-based Management*, vol. 1, no. 3, pp. 67–88, 2005.

[77] B. Honig and T. Karlsson, *Business Planning and the Nascent Entrepreneur: An Empirical Study of Normative Behavior*, Jönköping International Business School, Jönköping, 2001.

[78] B. Honig and T. Karlsson, "Institutional forces and the written business plan," *Journal of Management*, vol. 30, no. 1, pp. 29–48, 2004.

[79] B. Honig and T. Karlsson, "Nascent entrepreneurship in Sweden and the USA: An empirical examination contrasting representation with realization," Paper presented at the conference: Nascent Entrepreneurship: The Hidden Potential (CD), Durham, 2005.

[80] S. E. Human and C. H. Matthews, "Future expectations for the new business," In: *Handbook of Entrepreneurial Dynamics: The Process of Business Creation*, Gartner, W. B., Shaver, K. G., Carter, N. M., and Reynolds, P. D., Sage, Thousand Oakes, pp. 386–400, 2004.

[81] B. Jovanovic, "Selection and the evolution of industry," *Econometrica*, vol. 50, no. 3, pp. 649–670, 1982.

[82] D. Kahneman and A. Tversky, "Prospect Theory: An analysis of decisions under risk," *Econometrica*, vol. 47, pp. 263–279, 1979.

[83] J. Katz and W. B. Gartner, "Properties of emerging organizations," *Academy of Management Review*, vol. 13, no. 3, pp. 429–441, 1988.

[84] P. H. Kim, H. A. Aldrich, and L. A. Keister, "If I were rich? The impact of financial and human capital on becoming a nascent entrepreneur," Paper presented at the Annual Meeting of the American Sociological Association, Atlanta, 2003.

[85] P. H. Kim and H. E. Aldrich, "Teams that work together, stay together: Resiliency of entrepreneurial teams (Summary)," Paper presented at the Babson College/Kauffman Foundation Entrepreneurship Research Conference, Strathclyde, Scotland, 2004.

[86] G. King and L. Zeng, "Logistic regression in rare events data," *Political Analysis*, vol. 9, no. 2, pp. 137–163, 2001.

[87] I. M. Kirzner, *Competition and Entrepreneurship*, University of Chicago Press, Chicago, IL, 1973.

[88] P. Köllinger and M. Minniti, "Not for lack of trying: American entrepreneurship black and white," Paper presented at the conference: Nascent Entrepreneurship: The Hidden Potential (CD), Durham, 2005.

[89] J. Kruger and P. Dunning, "Unskilled and unaware of it: How difficulties in recognizing one's own incompetence leads to inflated self-assessments," *Journal of Personality and Social Psychology*, vol. 77, no. 6, pp. 1121–1134, 1999.

[90] K. Lewin, T. Dembo, L. Festinger, and P. S. Sears, "Level of aspiration," In: *Personality and Behavior Disorders*, McHunt, J., vol. 1, Ronald Press Company, New York, pp. 335–378, 1944.

[91] J. Liao and H. Welsch, "The temporal patterns of venture creation process: An exploratory study," In: *Frontiers of Entrepreneurship Research 2002*, Bygrave, W. D. *et al.*, Babson College, Wellesley, MA, 2002.

[92] J. Liao and H. Welsch, "Exploring the venture creation process: Evidence from tech and non-tech nascent entrepreneurs," In: *Frontiers of Entrepreneurship Research 2003*, Bygrave, W. D. *et al.*, Babson College, Wellesley, MA, 2003.

[93] J. Liao and H. Welsch, "Social capital and entrepreneurial growth aspiration: a comparison of technology- and non-technology-based nascent entrepreneurs," *Journal of High Technology Management Research*, vol. 14, pp. 149–170, 2003.

[94] B. B. Lichtenstein, N. M. Carter, K. Dooley, and W. B. Gartner, "Exploring the temporal dynamics of organizational emergence (Summary)," Paper presented at the Babson College/Kauffman Foundation Entrepreneurship Research Conference, Strathclyde, Scotland, 2004.

[95] B. B. Lichtenstein, K. Dooley, and G. T. Lumpkin, "Measuring emergence in the dynamics of new venture creation," *Journal of Business Venturing*, 2005, in press.

[96] C. H. Matthews, M. W. Ford, and S. E. Human, "The context of new venture initiation: Comparing growth expectations of nascent entrepreneurs and intrapreneurs," In: *Frontiers of Entrepreneurship 2001*, Bygrave, W. D. *et al.*, Babson College, Wellesley, MA, 2001.

[97] C. H. Matthews and S. E. Human, "The little engine that could: Uncertainty and growth expectations of nascent entrepreneurs," In: *Frontiers of Entrepreneurship Research 2000*, Reynolds, P. D. *et al.*, Babson College, Wellesley, MA, 2000.

[98] A. M. McCarthy, F. D. Schoorman, and A. C. Cooper, "Reinvestment decisions by entrepreneurs: Rational decision making or escalation of commitment," *Journal of Business Venturing*, no. 8, pp. 9–24, 1993.

[99] A. L. Mok and H. van den Tillaart, "Farmers and small businessmen: A comparative analysis of their careers and occupational orientation," In: *New Findings and Perspectives in Entrepreneurship*, Donckels, R. and Miettinen, A., Avebury, Aldershot, UK, pp. 203–230, 1990.

[100] B. O. Muthén, "Latent variable modeling of longitudinal and multilevel data," In: *Sociological Methodology*, Raftery, A., Blackwell Publishers, Boston, MA, 1997.

[101] B. O. Muthén and P. J. Curran, "General longitudinal modeling of individual differences in experimental designs: A latent variable framework for analysis and power estimation," *Psychological Methods*, vol. 2, no. 4, pp. 371–402, 1997.

[102] S. L. Newbert, "New firm formation: A dynamic capability perspective," *Journal of Small Business Management*, vol. 43, no. 1, pp. 55–77, 2005.

[103] S. Parker and Y. Belghitar, "What happens to nascent entrepreneurs? An econometric analysis of the PSED," Paper presented at the First Annual Clemson/Kauffman Symposium on the PSED, Clemson, SC, 2004.

[104] P. D. Reynolds, "Who starts new firms? Preliminary explorations of firms-in-gestation," *Small Business Economics*, vol. 9, pp. 449–462, 1997.

[105] P. D. Reynolds, "National panel study of US business start-ups. Background and methodology," In: *Advances in Entrepreneurship, Firm Emergence and Growth*, Katz, J. A., vol. 4, JAI Press, Stamford, CT, pp. 153–227, 2000.

[106] P. D. Reynolds, N. Bosma, E. Autio, S. Hunt, N. De Bono, and I. *et al.* Servais, "Global entrepreneurship monitor: Data collection design and implementation 1998–2003," *Small Business Economics*, vol. 24, pp. 205–231, 2005.

[107] P. D. Reynolds, W. D. Bygrave, and E. Autio, *GEM 2003 Global Report*, Kauffman Foundation, Kansas, MO, 2003.

[108] P. D. Reynolds, W. D. Bygrave, E. Autio, L. Cox, and M. Hay, *GEM Global 2002 Executive Report*, Kauffman Foundation, Kansas MO, 2002.

[109] P. D. Reynolds, S. M. Camp, W. D. Bygrave, E. Autio, and M. Hay, *Global Entrepreneurship Monitor. 2001 Executive Report*, Kauffman Foundation, Kansas MO, 2001.

[110] P. D. Reynolds, M. Hay, W. D. Bygrave, S. M. Camp, and E. Autio, *GEM 2000 Executive Report*, Kauffman Foundation, Kansas, MO, 2000.

[111] P. D. Reynolds, M. Hay, and S. M. Camp, *Global Entrepreneurship Monitor: 1999 Executive Report*, Kauffman Foundation, Kansas, MO, 1999.

[112] P. D. Reynolds and B. Miller, "New firm gestation: Conception, birth and implications for research," *Journal of Business Venturing*, vol. 7, pp. 405–417, 1992.

[113] P. D. Reynolds, D. J. Storey, and P. Westhead, "Cross-national comparisons of the variation in new firm formation rates," *Regional Studies*, vol. 28, no. 4, pp. 443–456, 1994.

[114] P. D. Reynolds and S. B. White, "Finding the nascent entrepreneur: Network sampling and entrepreneurship gestation," In: *Frontiers of Entrepreneurship Research 1992*, Churchill, N. C., Birley, S., Bygrave, W. D., Wahlbin, C., and Wetzel, W. E. J., pp. 199–208, Babson College, Wellesley, MA, 1992.

[115] H. O. Rocha and R. Sternberg, "Entrepreneurship: The role of clusters. Theoretical perspectives and empirical evidence from Germany," *Small Business Economics*, vol. 24, pp. 267–292, 2005.

[116] B. Rotefoss and L. Kolvereid, "Aspiring, nascent and fledgling entrepreneurs: An investigation of the business start-up process," *Entrepreneurship and Regional Development*, vol. 17, no. 2, pp. 109–127, 2005.

[117] M. Ruef, H. E. Aldrich, and N. M. Carter, "The structure of organizational founding teams: Homophily, strong ties, and isolation among U.S. entrepreneurs," *American Sociological Review*, vol. 68, no. 2, pp. 195–222, 2003.

[118] M. S. Salimath, J. B. Cullen, and K. P. Parboteeah, "A cross national study of entrepreneurial activity: Effects of the cultural and institutional context," Paper presented at the Babson College/Kauffman Foundation Entrepreneurship Research Conference, Wellesley, MA, 2005.

[119] M. Samuelsson, "Modeling the nascent venture opportunity exploitation process across time," In: *Frontiers of Entrepreneurship Research 2001*, Bygrave, W. D., Autio, E., Brush, C. G., Davidsson, P., Greene, P. G., Reynolds, P. D., and Sapienza, H. J., Wellesley, MA, pp. 66–79, 2001.

[120] M. Samuelsson, *Creating New Ventures: A Longitudinal Investigation of the Nascent Venturing Process*, Doctoral dissertation, Jönköping International Business School, Jönköping, 2004.

[121] S. Sarasvathy, "Causation and effectuation: Towards a theoretical shift from economic inevitability to entrepreneurial contingency," *Academy of Management Review*, vol. 26, no. 2, pp. 243–288, 2001.

[122] S. Sarasvathy, "Entrepreneurship as the science of the artificial," *Journal of Economic Psychology*, vol. 24, no. 203–220, pp. 203–220, 2002.

[123] S. Sarasvathy, N. Dew, R. Velamuri, and S. Venkataraman, "Three views of entrepreneurial opportunity," In: *Handbook of Entrepreneurship Research*, Acs, Z. J. and Audretsch, D. B., Kluwer, Dordrecht, NL, 2003.

[124] J. L. Schafer and J. W. Graham, "Missing data: Our view of the state of the art," *Psychological Methods*, vol. 7, no. 2, pp. 147–177, 2002.

[125] S. Scheinberg and I. C. MacMillan, "An 11 country study of motivations to start a business," In: *Frontiers of Entrepreneurship Research 1988*, Kirchhoff, B. A., Long, W. A., McMullan, W. E., Vesper, K. H., and Wetzel, W. E., Babson College, Wellesley, MA, pp. 669–687, 1988.

[126] T. Schoett and T. Bager, "Growth expectations by entrepreneurs in nascent firms, baby businesses and mature firms," In: *The Growth of Danish Firms. Part 2 of The Global Entrepreneurship Monitor, Denmark 2003*, Bager, T. and Hancock, M., Boersens, Copenhagen, pp. 219–230, 2004.

[127] S. Shane, "Prior knowledge and the discovery of entrepreneurial opportunities," *Organization Science*, vol. 11, no. 4, pp. 448–469, 2000.

[128] S. Shane and F. Delmar, "Planning for the market: Business planning before marketing and the continuation of organizing efforts," *Journal of Business Venturing*, vol. 19, pp. 767–785, 2004.

[129] S. Shane and S. Venkataraman, "The promise of entrepreneurship as a field of research," *Academy of Management Review*, vol. 25, no. 1, pp. 217–226, 2000.

[130] A. Shapero and L. Sokol, "The social dimension of entrepreneurship," In: *The Encyclopedia of Entrepreneurship*, Kent, C. A., Sexton, D. L., and Vesper, K. H., Prentice-Hall, Englewood Cliffs, NJ, pp. 72–90, 1982.

[131] K. G. Shaver, N. M. Carter, W. B. Gartner, and P. D. Reynolds, "Who is a nascent entrepreneur? Decision rules for identifying and selecting entrepreneurs in the panel study of entrepreneurial dynamics (PSED) [summary]," In: *Frontiers of Entrepreneurship Research 2001*, Bygrave, W. D., Autio, E., Brush, C. G., Davidsson, P., Greene, P. G., Reynolds, P. D., and Sapienza, H. J., Babson College, Wellesley, MA, pp. 122, 2001.

[132] B. Smith, "The search for and discovery of different types of entrepreneurial opportunities: The effects of tacitness and codification," Paper presented at the Babson College/Kauffman Foundation Entrepreneurship Research Conference, Wellesley, MA, 2005.

[133] N. R. Smith, *The Entrepreneur and His Firm: The Relationship Between Type of Man and Type of Company*, Michigan State University, East Lansing, MI, 1967.

[134] J. Stanworth, S. Blythe, B. Granger, and C. Stanworth, "Who becomes an entrepreneur?," *International Small Business Journal*, vol. 8, pp. 11–22, 1989.

[135] A. Stel, M. Carree, and A. R. Thurik, "The effect of entrepreneurial activity on national economic growth," *Small Business Economics*, vol. 24, pp. 311–321, 2005.

[136] R. Sternberg and S. Wennekers, "Determinants and effects of new business creation using Global Entrepreneurship Monitor data," *Small Business Economics*, vol. 24, pp. 193–203, 2005.

[137] J. Timmons, *New Venture Creation: Entrepreneurship for the 21st Century*, Irwin/McGraw-Hill, Boston, 1999.

[138] A. H. van de Ven, S. Venkataraman, D. Polley, and R. Garud, "Processes of new business creation in different organizational settings," In: *Research on the Management of Innovation: The Minnesota Studies*, van de Ven, A. H., Angle, H., and Poole, M. S., Harper/Ballinger, New York, pp. 222–226, 1989.

[139] M. van Gelderen, N. Bosma, and A. R. Thurik, "Setting up a business in the Netherlands: Who starts, who gives up, who is still trying?," In: *Frontiers of Entrepreneurship Research 2001*, Bygrave, W. D. *et al.*, Babson College, Wellesley, MA, 2001.

[140] M. Van Gelderen, A. R. Thurik, and N. Bosma, "Success and risk factors in the pre-startup phase," *Small Business Economics*, vol. 24, pp. 365–380, 2005.

[141] S. Venkataraman, "Some methodological challenges for entrepreneurial process research," Symposium paper presented at the Academy of Management meeting, Cincinnati, August, 1996.

[142] I. Verheul and A. R. Thurik, "Explaining the entrepreneurial activity rate of women: A macro-level perspective," SCALES Paper N200304, EIM, Zoetermeer, NL, 2003.

[143] J. Wagner, "Testing Lazear's jack-of-all-trades view of entrepreneurship with German micro data," *Applied Economic Letters*, vol. 10, pp. 687–689, 2003.

[144] J. Wagner, "Are young and small firms hothouses for nascent entrepreneurs?," *Applied Economics Quarterly*, vol. 50, no. 4, pp. 379–391, 2004.

[145] J. Wagner, *Nascent Entrepreneurs. IZA DP No. 1293*, Forschungsinstitut zur Zukunft der Arbeit, Bonn, Germany, 2004.

[146] J. Wagner, *What a Difference a Y Makes – Female and Male Nascent Entrepreneurs in Germany. IZA DP No. 1134*, Forschungsinstitut zur Zukunft der Arbeit, Bonn, Germany, 2004.

[147] J. Wagner, "Nascent and infant entrepreneurs in Germany: Evidence from the Regional Entrepreneurship Monitor (REM)," Paper presented at the Nascent Entrepreneurship: The Hidden Potential (CD), Durham, 2005.

[148] J. Wagner and R. Sternberg, "Start-up activity, industrial characteristics and the regional milieu: Lessons for entrepreneurship support policy from German microdata," *Annals of Regional Science*, vol. 38, pp. 219–240, 2004.

[149] F. Welter, "Who wants to grow? Growth intentions and growth profiles of (nascent) entrepreneurs in Germany," In: *Frontiers of Entrepreneurship Research 2001*, Bygrave, W. B. *et al.*, Babson College, Wellesley, 2001.

[150] S. Wennekers, A. Stel, A. R. Thurik, and P. D. Reynolds, "Nascent entrepreneurship and the level of economic development," *Small Business Economics*, vol. 24, pp. 293–309, 2005.

[151] P. Westhead and M. Wright, "Novice, portfolio, and serial Founders: Are they different?," *Journal of Business Venturing*, vol. 13, pp. 173–204, 1998.

[152] J. Wiklund, "The sustainability of the entrepreneurial orientation – performance relationship," *Entrepreneurship Theory and Practice*, vol. 24, no. 1, pp. 37–48, 1999.

[153] J. Wiklund, P. Davidsson, and F. Delmar, "What do they think and feel about growth? An expectancy-value approach to small business managers' attitudes towards growth," *Entrepreneurship Theory and Practice*, vol. 27, no. 3, pp. 247–269, 2003.

[154] J. Wiklund and D. Shepherd, "Aspiring for, and achieving growth: the moderating role of resources and opportunities," *Journal of Management Studies*, vol. 40, no. 8, pp. 1911–1941, 2003.

[155] P. W. Wong, Y. P. Ho, and E. Autio, "Entrepreneurship, innovation and economic growth: Evidence from GEM data," *Small Business Economics*, vol. 24, pp. 335–350, 2005.

[156] C. Y. Woo, A. C. Cooper, and W. C. Dunkelberg, "The development and interpretation of entrepreneurial typologies," *Journal of Business Venturing*, vol. 6, no. 2, pp. 93–114, 1991.

Foundations and Trends® in Entrepreneurship

Volume 2 Issue 1, 2006

Editorial Board

Editorial Scope

Foundations and Trends® in Entrepreneurship will publish survey and tutorial articles in the following topics:

- Nascent and start-up entrepreneurs
- Opportunity recognition
- New venture creation process
- Business formation
- Firm ownership
- Market value and firm growth
- Franchising
- Managerial characteristics and behavior of entrepreneurs
- Strategic alliances and networks
- Government programs and public policy
- Gender and ethnicity
- New business financing:
  - Business angels
  - Bank financing, debt, and trade credit
  - Venture capital and private equity capital
  - Public equity and IPO's
- Family-owned firms
- Management structure, governance and performance
- Corporate entrepreneurship
- High technology:
  - Technology-based new firms
  - High-tech clusters
- Small business and economic growth

Information for Librarians

Foundations and Trends® in Entrepreneurship, 2006, Volume 2, 4 issues. ISSN paper version 1551-3114 (USD 300 N. America; EUR 300 Outside N. America). ISSN online version 1551-3122 (USD 300 N. America; EUR 300 Outside N. America). Also available as a combined paper and online subscription (USD 340 N. America; EUR 340 Outside N. America).

Foundations and Trends® in
Entrepreneurship
Vol 2, No 1 (2006) 1-76
© 2006 P. Davidsson

Nascent Entrepreneurship: Empirical Studies and Developments

Per Davidsson

Brisbane Graduate School of Business, QUT, Australia and Jönköping International Business School, Sweden, per.davidsson@qut.edu.au

Abstract

The key ideas behind the empirical study of 'nascent entrepreneurship' are that the research aims to identify a statistically representative sample of on-going venture start-up efforts and that these start-up efforts are subsequently followed over time so that insights can be gained also into process issues and determinants of outcomes. The purpose of this paper is to take stock of the developments of 'nascent entrepreneur' – or 'firm gestation' – research so far, and to suggest directions for future research efforts along those lines. For this purpose a review has been made of some 75 journal articles, various book chapters, conference papers and research reports.

The review shows that the current approach to capturing on-going start-up efforts and studying their concurrent development longitudinally is a basically sound, workable approach that has opened up a new and very promising avenue for entrepreneurship research. While many interesting results have already been reported and while considerable improvements on both the method and theory sides of research have been made, there is still room and need for further improvements. A set of 17 specific propositions is developed towards that end.